A Quick Guide to Learning Python

Easy Coding, Designed for Beginners

ISBN: 978-9083404936
Paperback

Table of Contents

What Does This Book Cover?

Mastering a programming language requires understanding code and writing it effectively. This book offers quizzes to improve skills in reading and understanding code, while the exercises aim to improve writing code skills.

Each chapter starts with an explanation and code examples and is followed by exercises and quizzes, offering an opportunity for self-testing and understanding which level you achieved.

This book goes beyond the traditional approach by explaining Python syntaxes with real-world code examples. This approach makes learning exciting and ensures readers can apply their knowledge effectively. The included exercises and quizzes, along with their solutions, provide a guarantee to readers and empower them to create simple yet valuable programs.

Learning one computer language facilitates learning other computer languages. This principle arises from rules and logic that connect computer languages. A confirmation of this was when I was asked to teach the C# programming language at the University of Applied Science. Despite having no experience with C#, I dedicated a weekend to diving into the language and realized it wasn't fundamentally different from other object-oriented programming languages.

Python is also a language reliant on object-oriented programming principles. Our focus is real-world examples, enabling you to apply these concepts in your programming works. Learning programming is a communication tool with computers, as machines operate using their language defined by specific logical structures and sentences known as statements.

Before starting with the chapters, I present some illustrative code examples to provide an overview of the content of this book. The code at the beginning of this book gives you an idea about this book's approach.

How to get the most out of this book?

This book aims to teach Python to beginners with no programming background, but it is also practical for people who want to improve their knowledge.

1. People who don't have any programming background.

- Following the first step, it is recommended that you install Python 3 or later and an IDE to write and run the code.
- For each chapter, test yourself with the quizzes and the exercises that belong to the chapter. If your level of making the quizzes and the exercises is less than 50 percent, go back to the chapter's explanation and code examples to understand the current chapter before starting with the next one.
- The knowledge offered in Chapter 1 is necessary and will be included in the second chapter. The knowledge provided in the first and the second chapters is required in the third chapter, etc.
- There are many practical programming codes in this book. If you finish this book and learn more than 50% of the offered knowledge, you can work further with Python without needing a teacher. Remember, even experts maintain their knowledge continuously. I don't mean that you don't need to learn anymore, but you can learn further independent of teachers or instructors.

2. People with some background in Python programming or other programming language.

- You can start from the very beginning. I assume you have already worked with IDEs, and installing the development environment wouldn't be an issue.
- Before skipping any chapters, ensure you answer the quizzes and the exercises of the chapter. Once you solve them, you can skip that chapter. Otherwise, I recommend studying the chapter's explanation

and the example code to understand the chapter's topics before going further with the following chapters.

Sar Maroof

Is This Book Right for You?

In learning any programming language, it's crucial to emphasize two fundamental principles: reading and writing code. This book is designed to enable an understanding of code by explaining each chapter and providing numerous code examples.

At the end of every chapter, you'll find quizzes and exercises. Quizzes are a valuable test of your ability to read and understand code, while exercises test your ability to write Python code. If you have difficulties solving the quizzes and the exercises in any chapter, consider it an indication to dedicate more time to reading and learning the given examples. However, you can also read the solutions, which provide explanations and make it easy to understand.

It's important to note that, as a beginner, you're not expected to answer the following sample quizzes and exercises. Instead, they are included to give you an idea regarding the book's instructional approach.

Why Choose a Text-Based Application?

For beginners, it is crucial to start by learning coding in a text-based application. This approach allows you to focus on the fundamentals without dealing with the complexities of a graphical user interface. After Learning coding with text-based applications, you can independently explore graphical interfaces through tutorials or any preferred learning method.

Sample of the Quizzes and the Exercises

1 Create a Triangle

CH 4: Example 2

Write a program that asks the user to enter a character. Once the user inserts the character and presses the Enter button, the program draws a triangle with the entered symbol, as shown below.

In this output, the user enters the number "8", and the program draws a triangle with the number.

Output of the code

```
Enter a character: 8
8
88
888
8888
88888
888888
8888888
```

In this output, the user enters the character "$," and the program draws a triangle with the dollar symbol.

Output of the code

```
Enter a character: $
$
$$
$$$
$$$$
$$$$$
$$$$$$
$$$$$$$
```

The solution(s) of this code issue and its explanation, including many more, are covered in this book.

2 Secret Number

CH 5: Example 2A

Write a program that allows users to guess a secret number from 1 to 10. If the user's guess number is correct, the program confirms that the guess number is correct; otherwise, it is incorrect.

Output 1: The user enters the number 5 in the following output.

```
Guess a number from (1 to 10): 5
Number 5 is incorrect
```

Output 2: The user enters the number 8 in the following output.

```
Guess a number from (1 to 10): 8
Number 8 is correct
```

The solution(s) of this code issue and its explanation, including many more, are covered in this book.

3 Convert Euro to Dollar

CH 5: Exercise 1

Create a program that enables users to enter a specified amount in Euros, and the program should then convert this amount into dollars, considering the exchange rate of 1 Euro is equivalent to $1.10.

Output 1: The user enters an amount of 100 euro

```
Enter an amount in Euros: 100
The amount of 100.0 is $110.00
```

Output 2: The user enters an amount of 120 euro

```
Enter an amount in Euros: 120
The amount of 120.0 is $132.00
```

The solution(s) of this code issue and its explanation, including many more, are covered in this book.

4 Create an English Dictionary

CH 8: Exercise 1

Write a program that allows users to enter an English word; the program displays a synonym of the word. Remember that the user could write the word all in uppercase, lowercase, or a combination of both. The program should find the synonymous if it exists in the dictionary regardless of the cases.

dictionary.py

```
eng_dictionary = {'Happy': 'Pleased', 'Fast': 'Quick', 'Big':
'Large', 'Smart': 'Clever'}

# add your code here
```

Output 1: The user enters the word "HAPPY"

```
Enter an English word: HAPPY
The synonymous of the word Happy is Pleased
```

Output 2: The user enters the word "fast"

```
Enter an English word: fast
The synonymous of the word Fast is Quick
```

Output 3: The user enters the word "bIG"

```
Enter an English word: biG
The synonymous of the word Big is Large
```

The solution(s) of this code issue and its explanation, including many more, are covered in this book.

5 Lottery

CH 11: Exercise 1

Create a program allowing users to shuffle the names in the list below. Upon executing the program, the names order is selected randomly. The winners are determined based on the following ranking:

- The first randomly selected name wins one million dollars.
- The second chosen random name wins 500 thousand dollars.

- The third randomly selected name wins 100 thousand dollars.

lottery.py

```
from random import shuffle
names = ["Emma", "David", "Jack", "George", "Ronald", "Vera",
"Bruce"]


# add the rest of your code here.
```

The output of the program is shown below. Remember that the winners will be randomly different each time you run the program.

```
The names randomly:
 ['Vera', 'Emma', 'Bruce', 'Ronald', 'David', 'Jack', 'George']
The winner of one million dollars is: Vera
The winner of 500 thousand dollars is: Emma
The winner of 100 thousand dollars is: Bruce
```

The solution(s) of this code issue and its explanation, including many more, are covered in this book.

6 Copy Freelancers List

CH 7: Quiz 5

What happens if the following code is run?

freelancers.py

```
freelancers = ["Edward", "Jeff", "Robert", "John", "Daniel"]


freelancers2 = freelancers.copy()
freelancers2.sort()


print(freelancers2[1], freelancers[1])
```

Select the correct answer:

a. The code prints "Jeff Jeff" to the output.

b. The code prints "Edward Daniel" to the output.

c. The code prints "Edward Jeff" to the output.

d. The code prints "Daniel Edward" to the output.

e. The code prints nothing to the output.

The solution(s) of this code issue and its explanation, including many more, are covered in this book.

7 Select Cards

CH 11: Example 3B

The following program declares a list with the card elements and values. The choice function allows you to select a card randomly.

cards.py

```python
from random import choice
cards = ["clubs", "Diamonds", "Hearts", "Spades"]
card_value = ["Ace", 2, 3, 4, 5, 6, 7, 8, 9, 10, "Jack", "Queen",
"King"]
# add your code here
```

Output 1: By running the program, a card is selected randomly.

```
Randomly selected card:  Queen of Hearts
```

Output 2: By running the program, a card is selected randomly.

```
Randomly selected card:  3 of Hearts
```

Output 3: By running the program, a card is selected randomly.

```
Randomly selected card:  8 of Spades
```

The solution(s) of this code issue and its explanation, including many more, are covered in this book.

8 Registration Date

CH 12: Exercise 1

Upon registering on your website, the system automatically captures and saves the registration date and time. Develop a program that allows users to enter their names, and the program displays the user's name alongside the current registration date and time.

Output: The user enters Jack, and the program automatically prints the current date and time.

```
Enter your name: Jack
Jack's registration was recorded on
03/02/2024 At 07:35:33 PM
```

The solution(s) of this code issue and its explanation, including many more, are covered in this book.

9 Creating and Writing Into a File

CH 13: Quiz 2

When executing the following code, it generates the file 'MyFile.txt.' What content is readable inside the file?

file.py

```python
path_dir = "MyFile.txt"


file1 = open(path_dir, "w")
q1 = "In the middle of difficulties lies opportunities." # Einstein
q2 = "What we think, we become." # Buddha
file1.close()


file1 = open(path_dir, "w")
file1.write(q2)
file1.close()
```

Select all the correct answers:

a. The content of the file is only "quote1."

b. The content of the file is only "quote2."

c. The content of the file is "quote1" and "quote2."

d. The content of the file is empty.

e. The code causes an error.

The solution(s) of this code issue and its explanation, including many more, are covered in this book.

10 Function Calculator

CH 9: Quiz 1

What happens if the following code is run?

calculator.py

```
def calculator(nr1, nr2, nr3):    # line 1
    result = nr1 + nr2 - nr3      # line 2
    return result                 # line 3


print(calculator(22, 20, 10))    # line 4
```

Select the correct answer:

a. The code prints "22" to the output.

b. The code prints "20" to the output.

c. The code prints "32" to the output.

d. The code prints "52" to the output.

e. The code prints nothing to the output.

The solution(s) of this code issue and its explanation, including many more, are covered in this book.

1. A Beginner's Guide

It is recommended that you read this chapter if you are a total beginner in programming. In the following chapters, many programs are presented, and testing them by running them is essential. That gives you an idea of how running code and displaying the output of a program works.

Installing Python Version 3 or Later

Installing Python version 3 or later is crucial to run the programs in this book. Once you install Python, you can choose the IDE that works with your platform, Windows, Mac, Linux, etc.

Notice

You must first download and install Python before installing the IDE program. That would make the installation easier and avoid errors.

Installing IDE Platform for Python Programs

IDE is an Integrated development environment. Installing the right platform would help run the code and benefit the most from this book.
Many IDE programs help you to edit and write Python programs. Some are free, and others are paid; an example of a free IDE is Pycharm Community Edition. But there are also other alternatives.

After installing Python and the IDE, you can open the IDE Program, as shown in the following illustration. You can find the instructions on the IDE provider's website.

After installing your IDE successfully and opening it, you will see something as shown in the image below. Most of the IDE screens are divided into three areas.

- First area: In the upper left, you see your files with Python extensions such as "register.py."
- Second area: If you double-click on the file, the content of the file appears in the upper right area, called the editor, where you can write, edit, or update your code.
- Third area: This is the output area at the bottom of the screen; you can run the program by clicking on the green arrow at the top or on the left of the output area. Once you click the green arrow, also called the run button, the code output appears, as shown in the image below.

Notice

The buttons for running the program and others could differ from one IDE to another. For more information, read the instructions of the IDE provider.

The IDE Screen

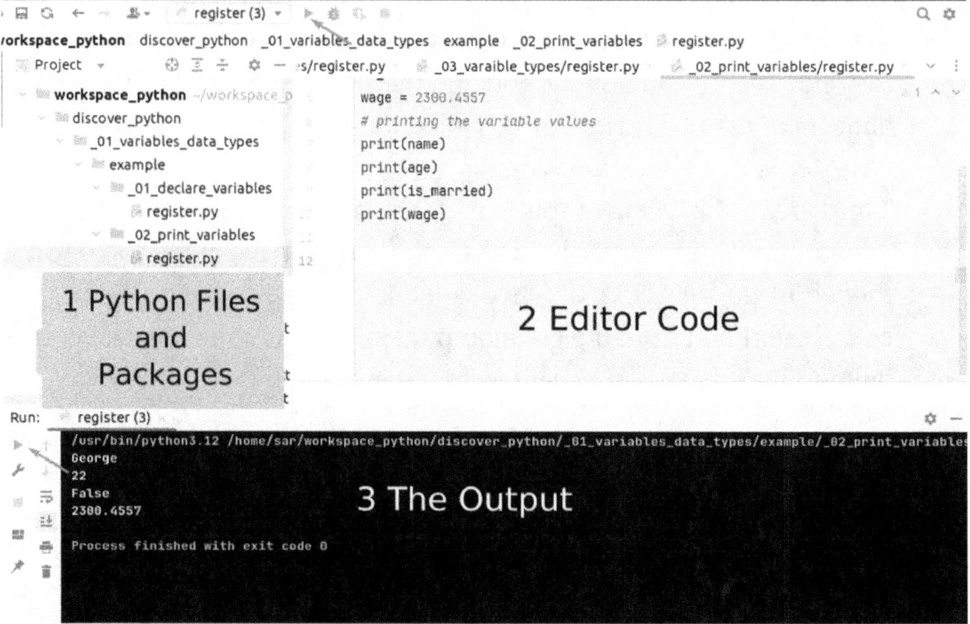

Check The Platform

Once you have installed Python and the IDE of your choice, follow the next steps to check whether the installation was successful.

- Create a Python file called register.py.
- Please type the code below in the editor area and write the code exactly as it is because Python is case-sensitive.
- Run the code by clicking on the green arrow.

Run the code of the following program, and if the output of the code is "George," that indicates the correctness of your installations.

file name: register.py

```python
name = "George"
```

```
print(name)
```

By clicking on the run button (green arrow), the name George appears in the output area, as shown below.

Output

```
George
```

Pythons Rules by Choosing Names

To maintain code readability, applying the following rules for naming variables, packages, modules, functions, and class names is essential.

Variables

Lowercase letters are used with words and separated by underscores. Examples are my_shopping_cart, bank_account, and user_age.

Packages (Modules) and Files

Lowercase letters are used with words and separated by underscores. Examples are brand.py, server_page.py, and data_source.py.

Functions (Methods)

Lowercase letters are used with words separated by underscores and ended by enclosed parenthesis. Examples, calculate_result(), get_sum().

2. Variables and Data Types

A variable allocates a location in the memory where you can store value. It is essential to give a variable a proper name or a reference that points to the memory location. The variable name is the key to accessing the memory's stored value.

Rules of Variable Names

Programmers can choose any proper names for variables but must apply the following rules.

- A variable name can only contain letters, numbers, and underscores.
- A variable name must start with a letter or with an underscore.
- Python is case-sensitive; therefore, "brand", "Brand", and "BRAND" differ.

Declaring Variables

In Python, creating variables is similar to other programming languages. It starts with the name of the variable and assigning a value to it.

Example 1: Creating Variables

The following code creates the variables name, age, is_married, and wage in the following example. Nothing will be printed in the output if you run the following code.

That is because the variables are declared, and values are assigned to them only in the memory. Programmers have control over when and where to display those data.

> **Notice**
>
> The string variable value should be enclosed in either single or double quotes, as demonstrated in the following example.

register.py

```python
# declaring variables
name = "George"
age = 22
is_married = False
wage = 2300.4557
```

Example 2: Printing the Variable Values

We expand the previous example by printing the variable values to the output.

To print variable values, we use the function print, which ends with opening parenthesis and closing it: print(). The variable's name should be passed as a parameter to the print function between the parenthesis, as shown in the example below.

The variable values are printed to the standard output if the following program is run.

register.py

```python
# declaring variables
name = "George"
age = 22
is_married = False
wage = 2300.4557
# printing the variable values
print(name)
print(age)
```

```
print(is_married)
print(wage)
```

Output of the previous code

```
George
22
False
2300.4557
```

Data Types

In programming, data type is an important concept.

Variables can be stored in different types. The primitive types examples are strings, a combination of letters, numbers, spaces, and symbols.

Numbers could be floats, numbers with decimals, and integers that represent numbers without decimals.

A boolean variable has only two possible values, either true or false.

The following are the primitive data types in Python; in Python, true and false start with uppercase letters, True and False.

Table 1: Data Types

Data Types	Acronym	Examples
String Type	str (string)	George, my text, How are you?
Integer Type	int (integer)	23, 45, 33
Decimal Type	float (decimal numbers)	34.343, 22. 3, 11.9
Boolean Type	bool (boolean)	True, False

Example 3: Data Types

The function type in Python allows you to print the types of the variables.

By using type(name), for example, the variable name data type is meant instead of the value of the name.

register.py

```python
# declaring variables
name = "George"
age = 22
is_married = False
wage = 2300.4557
# variable type
print(type(name))
print(type(age))
print(type(is_married))
print(type(wage))
```

As shown in the output, the variable type of name is a string (str), the variable type of age is an integer (int), the variable type of is_married is boolean (bool), and the variable type of wage is float, which is a number with a decimal.

Output

```
<class 'str'>
<class 'int'>
<class 'bool'>
<class 'float'>
```

Print By Using a Comma Operator

In Python, the comma(,) operator prints two or more expressions and separates them with a space.

Example 4A: Printing Texts

In the previous examples, we printed the value of the variables to the output. How can we display the data with more details, as shown below?

```
Name:      George
Age:       22
Married:   False
Wage:      2300.4557
```

To print a text, use the print function and enclose the text with double or single quotes, as shown below.

To print a combination of variable values and strings, you can separate them with a comma.

```python
# declaring variables
name = "George"
age = 22
is_married = False
wage = 2300.4557
'''
To print a combination of variable values and
texts, you can separate them with a comma.
'''

print("Name:     ", name)
print("Age:      ", age)
print("Married: ", is_married)
print("Wage:     ", wage)
```

Output

```
Name:      George
Age:       22
Married:   False
Wage:      2300.4557
```

Example 4B: Printing Texts

To print a combination with variable values and strings, you can separate them with a comma; by strings, they can also be separated by a plus sign (+), as shown in the code below.

```python
# declaring variables
name = "George"
age = 22
is_married = False
wage = 2300.4557
'''

To print a combination of variable values and
texts, you can separate them with a comma.
'''

# by name the sign + is used
print("Name:      "+ name)
print("Age:      ", age)
print("Married: ", is_married)
print("Wage:     ", wage)
```

Output

```
Name:       George
Age:        22
Married:    False
Wage:       2300.4557
```

Example 4C: Printing Texts

You can also enclose the text with a single quote, as shown in the code
below.

```python
# declaring variables
name = "George"
age = 22
is_married = False
wage = 2300.4557
'''

To print a combination of variable values and
texts, you can separate them with a comma.
'''

print('Name:       ', name)
print('Age:        ', age)
```

```
print('Married: ', is_married)
print('Wage:     ', wage)
```

Output

```
Name:     George
Age:      22
Married:  False
Wage:     2300.4557
```

Print Using Parameters "sep" and "end"

The "sep" Parameter

By default, a space is set between strings when separated by commas. However, there are situations where this default behavior is undesirable, and it is more practical to allow the programmer to determine the separation of characters. In such cases, the programmer can use the "sep" parameter to control the separation.

The "end" Parameter

The "end" parameter allows to print on the same line.

Example 4D: Printing Texts Using "sep" Parameter

In the following example, the "," creates a space between the dollar sign and the price by default. We can use the "sep" parameter to remove the space or add any character(s) between them.

```
wage = 2348.55
country = "United States"

print("Wage: $", wage)
'''
the sep="" specifies that no space or any other
characters are used between the dollar sign and the wage.
'''
```

```
print("Wage: $", wage, sep="")
print("Country", country)
'''

the sep=": " signifies the instruction to separate the
country and its corresponding value using a colon and a space.
'''

print("Country", country, sep=": ")
```

Output

```
Wage: $ 2348.55
Wage: $2348.55
Country United States
Country: United States
```

Example 4E: Printing Texts Using "end" Parameter

The following example shows that the "end" parameter keeps the word
"Country" and the variable value of the country, which is the United States,
on the same line.

```
country = "United States"
'''

the following statements print the
two words on two separate lines.
'''

print("Country")
print(country)
'''

Use the end parameter to ensure the two
words remain on the same line when printed.
'''

print("Country", end=": ")
print(country)
```

Output

```
Country
United States
```

```
Country: United States
```

Print By Using the 'f-String' Syntax

The 'f-string' syntax is an easy way of formatting strings in Python by prefixing the string with the letter f. This syntax allows you to print variable values using curly braces, as shown in the example below.

Example 5: Using f-String Syntax

The variable name between the curly braces prints the value of the variables.

```python
# declaring variables
name = "George"
age = 22
is_married = False
wage = 2300.4557


print(f"{name} is {age} years old.")
```

Output

```
George is 22 years old.
```

Example 6: Rounding to Two Decimal Places

There are several ways to round to less decimal places. In the following code, we used the first way by using the syntax "%.2f"

The second way uses the syntax ":.2f," which rounds to two decimal places. If you change the 2f to 3f, the decimal places become three.

```python
# declaring variables
```

```python
name = "George"
age = 22
is_married = False
wage = 2300.4557

# the first way to round to two decimal places
print("The wage of",name,"is: $%.2f" % wage+".")
# the second way to round to two decimal places
print(f"The wage is ${wage:.3f}.")
```

Output

```
The wage of George is: $2300.46.
The wage is $2300.456.
```

Using Comments

The interpreter ignores comments during the execution of the program. The primary usage of comments is to enhance the code's readability and explain the code to other programmers.

Python's two primary types of comments are single-line comments and multi-line comments.

A single-line comment starts with a hash (#), while a multi-line comment starts and is enclosed with a triple "single quote" or starts and is enclosed with a triple "double quote."

Why Are Comments Used in Python?

Every programming language supports comments as part of the language. Here below is an explanation of the crucial purposes of using comments.

1. Improve code readability for programmers.

2. Explaining the code to others who work with it.

3. Use the comments as solid documentation of the program.

4. Offering an easy and faster way to understand the functions of the code.

Example 7: Comments

The following code contains single and multiline comments.

register.py

```python
# this is a single-line comment.

'''
this is a multi-line comment
this is a multi-line comment
this is a multi-line comment
'''


"""
this is a multi-line comment
this is a multi-line comment
this is a multi-line comment
"""
```

Printing a String Multiple Times

In Python, multiplying a string by a number results in the string being repeated that number of times. An asterisk symbol serves as the multiplication operator.

Example 8: Multi-String

In the following example, we try to create a rectangle by multiplying a string by a number.

shape.py

```python
print('# ' * 10)
```

```
print('# ' * 10)
print('# ' * 10)
print('# ' * 10)
print('# ' * 10)
print('# ' * 10)
```

The output of the code is:

```
# # # # # # # # # #
# # # # # # # # # #
# # # # # # # # # #
# # # # # # # # # #
# # # # # # # # # #
# # # # # # # # # #
```

Type Casting

Type casting is converting one data type into another type. That is sometimes necessary because of the calculation or the operation that is required to be performed by the code. That can be accomplished in Python by using the functions int(), string(), float(), char(), bool(), etc.

Example 9A: Calculating Total Salary

In the following example, we calculate the total salaries earned by Jack and Emma. The expected output is $6000 because Jack earns $3200 and Emma earns $2800, but we get the error below when we run the program.

calculator.py

```
salary_Jack = 3200
salary_Emma = "2800"


total_salary = salary_Jack + salary_Emma
```

The output shows an error.

```
   total_salary = salary_Jack + salary_Emma
                   ~~~~~~~~~~~~^~~~~~~~~~~~~~
TypeError: unsupported operand type(s) for +: 'int' and 'str'
```

As shown in the output, the code causes an error because we tried to add the salary of 3200 to the wages of "2800". As shown in the code, double quotes enclose Emma's salary, which indicates that the wage is a string type, not a float type.

To solve the issue, we have to convert Emma's salary to a float using the function float, as shown below.

```
total_salary = salary_jack + float(salary_Emma)
```

Example 9B: Converting String to Float

The following code converts Emma's salary from a string to a float; otherwise, the program generates an error. Jack's wage is not enclosed with a double quote; therefore, it is already a number and doesn't need to be converted.

calculator.py

```
salary_Jack = 3200
salary_Emma = "2800"


total_salary = salary_Jack + float(salary_Emma)
print("Total salaries: $", total_salary)
```

Output

```
Total salaries: $ 6000.0
```

Example 9C: Converting String to Int

In the following example, to calculate the age difference between two individuals, you must convert the second age to int type because the second age is a string.

calculator.py

```python
age1 = 22
age2 = "34"

age_difference = int(age2) - age1
print("Age Difference: ", age_difference)
```

Output

```
Age Difference:  12
```

Escape Sequences in Python

Some characters are reserved as keywords in Python, such as double quotes, single quotes, backslash, etc. An escape sequence is a sequence of characters included within a string; it is transformed into a different character or set of characters, see the table below.

Table 2: Escape Sequences

Escape Sequence	Description
\\	Backslash
\'	Single quote
\"	Double quote
\n	New line
\t	Tab

Example 10: Escape sequence Code Example

```python
# print a double quote
print("He said, \"I am a student.\"")
# print a single quote
print('Who can tell me the meaning of the term \'ASCII\'?')
# print a backslash
print("The path of the program is C:\\Application\\color.py")
# new line
print("Hi There \nWelcome Back!")
# keep a tab between the texts
print("Name:\t David")
print("Age:\t 34")
```

The output of the program is:

```
He said, "I am a student."
Who can tell me the meaning of the term 'ASCII'?
The path of the program is C:\Application\color.py
Hi There
Welcome Back!
Name:  David
Age:    34
```

Quiz 1: Printing Variables

What happens if you run the following code?

course.py

```python
name = "C++"
duration = 3 # months
price = 3400.9574

print("%.2f" % price)
```

Select the correct answer:

a. The code prints "3400.9574" to the output.

b. The code prints "3400.96" to the output.

c. The code prints "float" to the output.

d. The code causes an error.

e. The code has no output.

Quiz 2: Printing Variables

What happens if you run the following code?

course.py

```
name = "C++"
duration = 3 # months
price = 3400.9574


print(type(name))
```

Select the correct answer:

a. The code prints "C++" to the output.

b. The code prints "3" to the output.

c. The code prints '<class 'str'>' to the output.

d. The code causes an error.

e. The code has no output.

Quiz 3: Total Weight in a Lift

What happens if you run the following code?

weight.py

```
weight1 = "80"
weight2 = 70
weight3 = "30"
total_weight = ""


print(total_weight)
```

What is the correct way to calculate the total weight in integer?

Select the correct answer:

a. total_weight = int(weight1) + weight2 + int(weight3)

b. total_weight = weight1 + int(weight2) + int(weight3)

c. total_weight = int(weight1) + int(weight2) + weight3

d. total_weight = weight1 + weight2 + weight3

e. The code has no output.

Quiz 4: Escape Sequences

What is the output of the code?

escape_sequence.py

```python
print("What does \'Database\' mean?")
```

Select the correct answer:

a. The output is "What does Database mean?"

b. The output is "What does \'Database\' mean?"

c. The output is "What does \Database\ mean?"

d. The output is "What does 'Database' mean?"

e. The code has no output.

Exercise 1: Printing Variable Values and Types

Print the values and the types of the variables brand, price, year, and is_defect, and round the price to two decimal places.

laptop.py

```python
brand = "Dell"
price = 2400.3572
year = 2030
is_defect = False
# add your code
```

The output of the program after adding your code is as shown below.

The expected output

```
The Variable Values
Brand:     Dell
Price:     $2400.36
Year:      2030
Is Defect?  False

The Variable Types
Type of brand is:     <class 'str'>
Type of price is:     <class 'float'>
Type of year is:      <class 'int'>
Type of is_defect is: <class 'bool'>
```

Exercise 2: Printing a shape

Use the multiplying string in Python to print the following triangle to the output.

```
U
U U
U U U
U U U U
U U U U U
U U U U U U
```

Answers to the Exercises

Answer Quiz 1

- The print function prints the price of the course.
- The syntax %.2f rounds the price to two decimal places. Therefore, the correct answer is b.

Output

```
3400.96
```

Answer Quiz 2

- Combining the print and the type function prints the variable's type, not its value. Therefore, the code writes a string type of the name's variable. The short name of a string in Python is "str."
- The correct answer is c.

Output

```
<class 'str'>
```

Answer Quiz 3

- The variable values of weight1 and weight3 are enclosed with double quotes. So, they are strings, and they need to be converted to integers.
- The variable weight2 is already an integer and doesn't need to be converted.
- The answer "a" calculates the total weight by converting weight1 and weight2 to an integer.
- The correct answer is a.

Output by replacing the statement total_weight =" " with the statement of the answer "a."

```
180
```

Answer Quiz 4

- The escape sequence \' prints a single quote; therefore, the output is "What does 'Database' mean?".
- The correct answer is d.

Output

```
What does  'Database' mean?
```

Answer Exercise 1

Here below is the answer to exercise 1.

```python
brand = "Dell"
price = 2400.3572
year = 2030
is_defect = False

print("The Variable Values")
print("Brand:      ", brand)
print("Price:       $%.2f" % price)
print("Year:       ", year)
print("Is Defect? ", is_defect)
print()
print("The Variable Types")
print("Type of brand is:     ", type(brand))
print("Type of price is:     ", type(price))
print("Type of year is:      ", type(year))
print("Type of is_defect is:", type(is_defect))
```

Output

```
The Variable Values
Brand:     Dell
Price:     $2400.36
Year:      2030
Is Defect?  False

The Variable Types
Type of brand is:     <class 'str'>
Type of price is:     <class 'float'>
Type of year is:     <class 'int'>
Type of is_defect is: <class 'bool'>
```

Answer Exercise 2

Below is the answer to exercise 2.

- First, print the letter U once, then twice, etc.

```
print('U ' * 1)
print('U ' * 2)
print('U ' * 3)
print('U ' * 4)
print('U ' * 5)
print('U ' * 6)
```

Output

```
U
U U
U U U
U U U U
U U U U U
U U U U U U
```

3. Operators in Python

There are several operator types in Python, such as arithmetic, assignment, comparison, logic, identity, and membership. The value that the operator operates on is called the operand.

Table 1: Arithmetic Operators

Arithmetic operators are used with numeric values to perform mathematical operations. The arithmetic operations include addition, subtraction, multiplication, division, and exponentiation. The operators, modulus, and floor division might be unknown to beginners.

Operator	Name	Example
+	Addition	7 + 2 = 9
-	Subtraction	7 - 2= 5
*	Multiplication	7 * 2 = 14
/	Division	7 / 2 = 3.5
**	Exponentiation	4 ** 2 = 4 * 4 * 4 = 64
%	Modulus	7 % 2 = 1
//	Floor division	7 // 2 = 3

Example 1: Arithmetic Operators

The following example code shows how to use arithmetic operations.

arithmetic.py

```
print(7 + 2)    # 9
print(7 - 2)    # 5
print(7 * 2)    # 7 * 2 = 14
print(7 / 2)    # 3.5
print(7 % 2)    # 1
print(4 ** 3)   # 4 * 4 * 4 = 64
print(17 // 2)  # 8
```

Output

Modulus

When a number is divided by another, the remainder is called modulus. The percentage symbol "%" represents modulus; see the following examples.

Examples

Operations	Explanation
10 % 3 = 1	10 divided by 3 = 3, and the remainder is 1
24 % 6 = 0	24 divided by 6 = 4, and the remainder is 0
21 % 8 = 5	21 divided by 8 = 2, and the remainder is 5.

Explanation

10 % 3 = 1	10 divided by 3 is 3. 3 * 3 = 9. remainder = 10 -9 = 1.
24 % 6 = 0	24 divided by 6 is 4. 6 * 4 = 24. remainder = 24 - 24 = 0.
21 % 8 = 5	21 divided by 8 is 2 2 * 8 = 16. remainder = 21 -16 = 5.

Example 2: Modulus

The following code clarifies how the modulus works.

modulus.py

```
print(10 % 3)   # remainder is 1
print(24 % 6)   # remainder is 0
print(21 % 8)   # remainder is 5
```

Output

```
1
0
5
```

Floor Division

The floor division is an arithmetic operation that divides a number by another, rounds the result to the integer, and ignores the remainder. The double slash symbol "//" is used for the floor division.

Examples

Operation	Explanation
30 // 4 = 7	30 divided by 4 = 7 4 * 7 = 28 the rest is 2 less than 7
22 // 5 = 4	22 divided by 5 = 4 4 * 5 = 20 the rest is 2 less than 5
20 // 4 = 5	20 divided by 4 = 5 5 * 4 = 20 the rest is 0
9 // 2 = 4	9 divided by 2 is 4 the rest is 1 less than 2
15 // 6 = 12	15 divided by 6 = 12 the rest is 3 less than 6.

Example 3: Floor Division

floor_division.py

```python
print(30 // 4) # 7
print(22 // 5) # 4
print(20 // 4) # 5
print(9 // 2)  # 4
print(15 // 6) # 2
```

Output

```
7
4
5
4
2
```

Table 2: Assignment Operators

The assignment operators are used to assign values to variables.

Operator	Example	Same as	Explanation
=	x = 7	x = 7	x is equal to 7
+=	x += 5	x = x + 5	Increment the value of x by 5
-=	x -= 4	x = x - 3	Decrement the value of x by 3
*=	x *= 2	x = x * 2	Multiply the value of x by 2
/=	x /= 4	x = x / 4	Divide the value of x by 4
%=	x %= 3	x = x % 3	x = x % 3
//=	x //= 2	x = x // 2	x = x // 2
**=	x ** 4	x = x ** 3	x to the power of 4

Example 4A: Assignment Operators

assignment.py

```python
nr1 = 3
nr2 = 4
nr3 = 5
nr4 = 12
nr5 = 8
nr6 = 5

nr1 += 5
print(nr1)   # prints 3 + 5 = 8

nr2 -= 3
print(nr2)   # prints 4 - 3 = 1

nr3 *= 2
print(nr3)   # prints 5 * 2 = 10

nr4 /= 3
print(nr4)   # prints 12 / 3 = 4

nr5 //= 5
print(nr5)   # prints 8 / 5 = 1

nr6 **= 3
print(nr6)   # prints 5 *  5 * 5 = 125
```

Output

```
8
1
10
4.0
1
125
```

Using the "+" and "+=" Operators With Strings

The following example shows you can concatenate separate strings with the "+" or "+=" operators.

Example 4B: Concatenate Strings Using "+"

concatenate.py

```python
name1 = "Jack "
name2 = "David "
name3 = "Emma "
'''
You can concatenate the values of
the names by using the '+' operator.
'''
name = name1 + name2 + name3

print(name)
```

Output

```
Jack David Emma
```

Example 4C: Concatenate Strings Using "+="

concatenate.py

```python
name1 = "Jack "
name2 = "David "
name3 = "Emma "
'''
you can concatenate the names
by using the "+=" operator
'''
name1 += name2
name1 += name3
```

```
# the name values 2 and 3 are concatenated to name1
print(name1)
```

Output

```
Jack David Emma
```

Table 3: Comparison Operators

It is allowed to compare values with one another. The result of comparing the values is either true or false.

Operator	Name	Example
==	Equal	4 == 4 = true
!=	Not equal	4 != 4 = false
>	Greater than	7 > 5 = true
<	Less than	7 < 5 = false
>=	Greater than or equal to	9 >= 9 = true
<=	Les than or equal to	9 <= 7 = false

Example 5: Comparison Operators

The following code shows how the comparison operators work.

comparison.py

```
x = 4
y = 4
n = 7
z = 5
i = 9
k = 9
```

```
print(x == y)   # is x equal to y? True
print(x != y)   # is x unequal to y? False
print(n > z)    # is n greater than z? True
print(i >= k)   # is i greater or equal to k? True
print(i <= n)   # is i smaller or equal to n? False
```

Output

```
True
False
True
True
False
```

Table 4: Logical Operators

Logical operators are used to combine conditional statements.

Operator	Description
and	Returns True if both statements are true.
or	Returns True if one of the statements is true.
not	Reverse the result returns false if the result is true .

Examples

Operation	Explanation
4 == 4 and 3 > 2	The first condition returns true because four is equal to 4. The second condition also returns true because three is greater than 2. The result is "true" because both conditions return true.
8 >= 3 and 2 > 5	The first condition returns true because eight is greater or equal to 3. The second condition returns false because two is not greater than 5.

	The result is "false" because one of the conditions returns false.
8 >= 3 or 2 > 5	The first condition returns true because eight is greater or equal to 3. The second condition returns false because two is not greater than 5. The result is "true" because one of the conditions returns true. Remember that the result is true if only one condition returns true by the "or" operator.
not (8 >= 3 or 2 > 5	The result of the previous condition was true. By applying the 'not' operator, the outcome will be inverted to false."

Example 6: Logical Operators

logical.py

```python
x = 5
y = 8
z = 12

print(x < y and x == 5)        # prints True
print(z < y and x == 5)        # prints False
print(x < y or x == 5)         # prints True
print(x < y or x == 5)         # prints True
print (not(x > 8 or x == 5))   # prints False
```

Output

```
True
False
True
True
False
```

Table 5: Identity Operators

Identity operators compare whether the objects are the same with the exact memory location.

Operator	Description
is	Returns true if the variables are the same
is not	Returns true if the variables are not the same

Example 7: Identity Operators

The following code clarifies how identity operators work.

```python
name1 = "George"
name2 = "Jack"
name3 = name1

print(name1 is name2)        # False
print(name2 is name3)        # False
print(name1 == name3)        # True because name3 = name 1
print(name1 is not name2)    # True
```

Output of the code

```
False
False
True
True
```

Table 6: Membership Operators

Membership operators test if a sequence is presented in an object.

Operator	Description
in	Returns True if a sequence with the specified value is present in the object.
not in	Returns True if a sequence with the specified value is absent

in the object.

Example 8: Membership Operators

```
text = "In the middle of difficulty lies opportunity." # Einstein

print("difficulty" in text) # True "difficulty" is in the text.
print("we" in text)         # False "we" is not in the text.
print("price" not in text)  # True "price" is not in the text
```

Output

```
True
False
True
```

Quiz 1: Arithmetic Operator

What happens if the following code is run?

calculator.py

```
print(17 % 3 , 29 // 6 , 4 **2)
```

Select the correct answer:

a. The code prints "2 5 8" to the output.

b. The code prints "5 4 16" to the output.

c. The code prints "2 4 16" to the output.

d. The code causes an error.

e. The code has no output.

Quiz 2: Assignment Operators

What happens if the following code is run?

calculator.py

```python
x = 5

x += 3
x -= 2

print(x)
```

Select the correct answer:

a. The code prints "5" to the output.

b. The code prints "8" to the output.

c. The code prints "3" to the output.

d. The code prints "6" to the output.

e. The code causes an error.

f. The code has no output.

Quiz 3: Comparison Operators

What happens if the following code is run?

calculator.py

```python
x = 5
y = 6

print(x == y)
print(y >= x)
print(y != 3)
print(y <= 6)
print(y < 4)
```

Select the correct answer:

a. The code prints "False True True True False" to the output.

b. The code prints "False True False True False" to the output.

c. The code prints "False False False True True" to the output.

d. The code prints "True True True True False" to the output.

e. The code causes an error.

f. The code has no output.

Quiz 4: Logical Operators

What happens if the following code is run?

calculator.py

```
nr1 = 3
nr2 = 4
nr3 = 5

print(nr1 < nr2 and nr3 != 5)
print(nr1 < nr2 or nr3 != 5)
```

Select the correct answer:

a. The code prints "True True" to the output.

b. The code prints "False True" to the output.

c. The code prints "False False" to the output.

d. The code prints "True False" to the output.

e. The code causes an error.

f. The code has no output.

Quiz 5: Identity Operators

What happens if the following code is run?

color.py

```
brand1 = "IBM"
brand2 = "Dell"
brand3 = brand1

print(brand1 is brand2)
print(brand3 is brand1)
```

```
print(brand3 == brand1)
```

Select the correct answer:

a. The code prints "False True False" to the output.

b. The code prints "False True True " to the output.

c. The code prints "False False False" to the output.

d. The code prints "True True True" to the output.

e. The code prints "True False True" to the output.

f. The code has no output.

Quiz 6: Membership Operators

What happens if the following code is run?

color.py

```
colors = "blue, red, green, black, white, yellow"

print("YELLOW" in colors)
print("red" in colors)
```

Select the correct answer:

a. The code prints "True True" to the output.

b. The code prints "True False" to the output.

c. The code prints "False False" to the output.

d. The code prints "False True" to the output.

e. The code has no output.

Exercise 1: Search fruits

Write two statements that check whether the fruits "orange and grape " are on the list.

```
fruits = "apple, banana, orange, mango, strawberry"

# enter your code
```

Output: The code checks orange and grape.

```
Is orange on the list? The answer is: True
Is grape on the list? The answer is: False
```

Exercise 2: Applying for a Job

Write a code that determines whether candidates are accepted or rejected based on their years of experience. If the user's experience is five years or more, the user gets a positive result; otherwise, the answer is negative or rejected.

Output

```
Five years of experience. Is he accepted? True
Seven years of experience. Is he accepted? True
Four years of experience. Is he accepted? False
```

Answers to the Exercises

Answer Quiz 1

- The program prints the first 17 % 3 . 17 divided by 3 is 5, and the remainder is 2.
- The second part prints 29 // 6. 29 divided by 6 is 4, and the remainder is ignored.
- The third part is 4 ** 2, which means 4 * 4 = 16.

The correct answer is c.

Output

```
2 4 16
```

```
6
```

Answer Quiz 2

x = 5

- The initial value of the variable x is 5.
- x += 3 increments the value of x by 3 and it becomes 8.
- x -= 2 decrements the value of x by 2. Remember that the last value of the variable x is 8, not 5. So, 8 -2 = 6.

The correct answer is d.

Output

```
6
```

Answer Quiz 3

x =5, y = 6

- The first statement print(x == y) returns false because x is 5 and is not equal to y, which is 6.
- The second statement print(y >= 5) returns true because y is 6, and that is greater than x.
- The third statement, print(y != 3), returns true because y is 6, and it is not equal to 3.
- The fourth statement print (y <= 6). Remember that y is not smaller than 6, but it is equal to 6. Therefore, it returns true.
- The fifth statement print(y < 4) returns false because y is not smaller than 4.

The correct answer is a.

Output

```
False
True
```

```
True
True
False
```

Answer Quiz 4

nr1 = 3, nr2 = 4, nr3 = 5.

- The first statement print(nr1 < nr2 and nr3 != 5) checks whether nr1 is smaller than nr2, which is true, but the second one checks whether nr3 is not equal to 5, which is false. Using the logical operator "and," all the statements should return true; otherwise, the result will be false.

- The second statement print(nr1 < nr2 or nr3 != 5) is precisely the same as the previous statement, but this time, the logical operator "or" is used, and by using or if one statement returns true, the result is true.

The correct answer is b.

Output

```
False
True
```

Answer Quiz 5

brand1 = "IBM", brand2 = "Dell", brand 3 = brand1.

- The first statement print(brand1 is brand2) checks whether the two brands are identical; therefore, it returns false because they are not.

- The second statement print(brand3 is brand1) checks whether brand3 is brand1, which they are, and they point to the exact location in the memory because the statement brand3 = brand1 is mentioned at the beginning of the code.

- The third statement, print(brand3 == brand1), checks whether brand3 equals brand1, which is true.

The correct answer is b.

Output

```
False
True
True
```

Answer Quiz 6

colors = "blue, red, green, black, white, yellow"

- The first statement print("YELLOW" in colors) checks whether the color "YELLOW" is in the list. Remember that Python is case-sensitive — "yellow" is not the same as "YELLOW", so the result is False.

- The second statement is print("red" in colors), which checks whether the color red is on the list and that is true.

The correct answer is d.

Output

```
False
True
```

Answer Exercise 1

fruit.py

```python
fruits = "apple, banana, orange, mango, strawberry"


print("Is orange on the list? The answer is:","orange" in fruits)
print("Is grape on the list? The answer is:","grape" in fruits)
```

Output

```
Is orange on the list? The answer is: True
Is grape on the list? The answer is: False
```

Answer Exercise 2

job.py

```
print("Five years of experience. Is he accepted?", 5 >= 5)
print("Seven years of experience. Is he accepted?", 7 >= 5)
print("Four years of experience. Is he accepted?", 4 >= 5)
```

Output

```
Five years of experience. Is he accepted? True
Seven years of experience. Is he accepted? True
Four years of experience. Is he accepted? False
```

4. User Input and Strings

User Input

In the previous chapters, we worked with variable values. In many cases, we don't have the values of the variables; instead, we need to ask the users to enter their data. Most well-known web applications ask users for their names, birthdates, occupations, etc.
You can also ask users in Python to enter their data using the function input(), as shown in the following examples.

Example 1: User Input

In this example, we allowed the user to enter his information and assign his data values to the variables we already declared for those data.

Notice

When you test the following program, the program first allows you to enter your first name. Each time you enter your data, you must press the enter button on your keyboard to insert the rest.

---

register.py

```python
'''
assign the values that the user enters to the
variables first name, last name, age, and occupation
'''


first_name = input("Enter your first name: ")
last_name = input("Enter your last name: ")
age = input("Enter your age:    ")
occupation = input("Enter your occupation: ")
# use "\n" for new line
print("\n..... Info of",first_name, last_name, ".....")
```

```python
# use \t for tab
print("Name: \t\t\t", first_name, last_name)

print("Age: \t\t\t", age)
print("Occupation: \t", occupation)
```

Output

```
Enter your first name: George
Enter your last name: Smith
Enter your age:   34
Enter your occupation: Programmer

..... Info of George Smith .....
Name:          George Smith
Age:           34
Occupation:    Programmer
```

Example 2: Create a Triangle

Write a program that asks the user to enter a character. Once the user inserts the character and presses the Enter button, the program draws a triangle with the entered symbol, as shown below.

In this output, the user enters the number "8", and the program draws a triangle with the number.

Output of the code

```
Enter a character: 8
8
88
888
8888
88888
888888
8888888
```

triangle.py

```python
symbol = input("Enter a character: ")

print(symbol * 1)
print(symbol * 2)
print(symbol * 3)
print(symbol * 4)
print(symbol * 5)
print(symbol * 6)
print(symbol * 7)
```

Example 3A: Calculate Weights

Three individuals try to use an elevator with a maximum weight capacity of
551 pounds (250 kg). The weights of the three individuals are as follows:
The first person weighs 199 pounds (90 kg).
The second person weighs 192 pounds (87 kg).
The third person weighs 177 pounds (80 kg).

Write a program that calculates the total weight of all three individuals and
informs them whether they can use the elevator simultaneously, considering
the maximum weight capacity.

calculator.py

```python
weight1 = input("Enter the weight of the first person: ")
weight2 = input("Enter the weight of the second person: ")
weight3 = input("Enter the weight of the third person: ")

# calculate the total weight
total_weight = weight1 + weight2 + weight3
print("The total weight is: ", total_weight, "pounds")
```

The program output is 199192177 pounds, as shown below, which is
incorrect.
Output of the program

```
Enter the weight of the first person: 199
```

```
Enter the weight of the second person: 192
Enter the weight of the third person: 177
The total weight is:  199192177 pounds
```

Earlier in this book, I explained that sometimes it is necessary to convert variable types from one type to another.

The output is "199192177", a combination of the three entered numbers by the user: 199, 192, and 177.

As explained before, the result of the sum of three strings is concatenating them together. Python considers the three numbers as strings.
Let's check the variable types of numbers entered by the user.

Example 3B: Checking the Variable Types

As I explained in this book, you can print any variable type in Python using the function type. To display it, you should use the function type combined with the print function as print(type(weight)), as shown in the code.

calculator.py

```python
weight1 = input("Enter the weight of the first person: ")
weight2 = input("Enter the weight of the second person: ")
weight3 = input("Enter the weight of the third person: ")

# check the variable types
print(type(weight1))
print(type(weight2))
print(type(weight3))

# calculate the total weight
total_weight = weight1 + weight2 + weight3
print("The total weight is: ", total_weight, "pounds")
```

It is clear from the output that Python sees all three variables, weight1, weight2, and weight3, as strings.

Output

```
Enter the weight of the first person: 199
Enter the weight of the second person: 192
Enter the weight of the third person: 177
<class 'str'>
<class 'str'>
<class 'str'>
The total weight is:  199192177 pounds
```

As already explained in this book, you can convert the string type in Python to an integer by using the function int as int(weight1), as shown in the code.

Example 3C: Converting Strings to Integers

In the following code, the string variables of weights are converted to integers. Therefore, the correct result is calculated by the program.

calculator.py

```python
weight1 = input("Enter the weight of the first person: ")
weight1 = input("Enter the weight of the first person: ")
weight2 = input("Enter the weight of the second person: ")
weight3 = input("Enter the weight of the third person: ")

# converting the variable from strings to integers
weight1 = int(weight1)
weight2 = int(weight2)
weight3 = int(weight3)

# calculate the total weight
total_weight = weight1 + weight2 + weight3
print("The total weight is: ", total_weight, "pounds")
```

The output clearly shows that the total weight is 568 pounds, which exceeds the maximum weight of 551 pounds allowed in the elevator.

Output

```
Enter the weight of the first person: 199
```

```
Enter the weight of the second person: 192
Enter the weight of the third person: 177
The total weight is:  568 pounds
```

> **Notice**
>
> The user input is a string, even if the user enters a number. Therefore, converting the input to an "int" type for integers or a "float" type for decimal numbers is crucial. Otherwise, the result of the arithmetic operation would be incorrect.

Strings and Substrings

There are many reasons for programmers to manipulate strings, such as limiting the number of characters a user enters for a comment, removing unwanted words in messages entered by users, finding a word or a sentence within a text, etc.

String Index

Each character within a string has a positive and negative index position number.
- The positive index starts with 0 from the left side.
- The negative index starts with -1 from the right side.

In the following book title, "Learn Java," each letter, including the space, has two different index position numbers, as shown below.

- The first letter, "L," has 0 and a negative index of -10.
- The letter "e" has a positive index number of 1 and a negative index of -9.
- The space has the indexes of 5 and -5.
- The letter "v" has the indexes 8 and -2.

title = "Learn Java"

The positive and the negative index number of each letter

0	1	2	3	4	5	6	7	8	9
L	e	a	r	n		J	a	v	a

-10	-9	-8	-7	-6	-5	-4	-3	-2	-1

We use the index number enclosed by brackets to determine each letter within a string.

For example, if we want to print the letter n of the title, we use the statement print(title[4]) or print(title[-6]) as shown in the following code.

Example 4: String Index

string_index.py

```python
title = "Learn Java"

print(title[0])      # prints L
print (title[-10])   # prints L
print (title[3])     # prints r
print(title[-7])     # prints r
print (title[8])     # prints v
print (title[-2])    # prints v
```

Output of the code

Substring

It is also possible to display a substring or a part of the string by indicating from which index position number to start and the end index position of the substring.

By printing a substring of a string, we also use the enclosed brackets; a colon separates the start and the end index ":" examples are title[6:9] and title[0:5].

In the previous example, we can separate the substring "Java" by determining the first index position number and leaving the end index position empty as title[6:]; it is also possible to use title[6:10].

> **Notice**
>
> The start index is inclusive, but the end index is exclusive. Therefore, we use the end index of 10, which doesn't exist but indicates excluding 10. It is recommended to leave it empty if you want to reach the end of the characters.

The positive and the negative index number of each letter

0	1	2	3	4	5	6	7	8	9
L	**e**	**a**	**r**	**n**		**J**	**a**	**v**	**a**
-10	-9	-8	-7	-6	-5	-4	-3	-2	-1

Example 5: Substring of a String

substring.py

```
title = "Learn Java"
'''
 if the end position is empty, it indicates
 reaching the end of the string.
'''
```

```python
print(title[6:])          # prints Java
print(title[6:10])        # prints Java
print (title[-4:])        # prints Java
print (title[-4:10])      # prints Java
'''

if the first position is empty, it indicates
starting from the beginning of the string
'''

print(title[:5])     # prints Learn
print(title[0:5])    # prints Learn
print(title[:-5])    # prints Learn
print(title[-10:5])  # prints Learn
'''

If both the initial and final positions
are empty, it implies the entire title.
'''

print(title[:])       # prints the whole title
print (title[0:10])   # prints the whole title
```

Output

```
Java
Java
Java
Java
Learn
Learn
Learn
Learn
Learn Java
Learn Java
```

Using Operators With Strings

As shown in the following examples, Python comparison operators could
also be used with strings such as "==" and "!=".

Example 6: Compare Strings

compare_strings.py

```python
# returns true
print("California" == "California")
# returns false, Python is case-sensitive
print("New York" == "New york")
# returns true, because they are not equal
print("United States" != "United states")
# returns false, the leftside lacks space between the words.
print("Hi" +"There" == "Hi There")
# returns true, space in the end of Hi
print("Hi " +"There" == "Hi There")
# returns true, space in the beginning of There
print("Hi" +" There" == "Hi There")
```

Output

```
True
False
True
False
True
True
```

Example 7A: Find Substrings Within a String

Write a program that enables users to search in a country list whether it contains the country they seek. The program's answer is "true" if the country is on the list. However, the program's answer would be false if the country is not on the list.

In the following output, the user seeks India, which is on the list. Therefore, the program's answer is "true."

```
Current List:  United States, United Kingdom, Germany, India, Brazil, Spain, Italy, Canada, Japan,
Mexico

Enter a country name: India
```

```
Is  India on the list?  True
```

In the following output, the user seeks France, which is not on the list. Therefore, the program's answer is "false".

```
Current List:  United States, United Kingdom, Germany, India, Brazil, Spain, Italy, Canada, Japan,
Mexico

Enter a country name: France
Is  France on the list?  False
```

Notice

The provided list represents the top 10 nations worldwide where, to date, my books are the most popular, ranked by their level of popularity.

Here below is the code.

find_country.py

```python
countries = "United States, United Kingdom, Germany, India,
Brazil, Spain, Italy, Canada, Japan, Mexico"
print("Current List: ", countries)
country = input("\nEnter a country name: ")


print("Is ", country, "on the list? ", country in countries)
```

The following challenge needs to be solved.

Challenge

If you enter an existing country on the list using different letter cases, the program's answer would be "false, " which is undesirable.

In the following output of the same previous code, the user enters "germany" starting with a lowercase, but the program mentions that "germany" is not on the list. That is because Python is case-sensitive.

```
Current List:  United States, United Kingdom, Germany, India, Brazil, Spain, Italy,
Canada, Japan, Mexico

Enter a country name: germany
Is  germany on the list?  False
```

Question

How can we instruct the program to disregard letter cases when the user enters input with incorrect casing?

The answer to the question is in the following topic of the string functions. That will teach you how to manipulate strings in that case and many others.

String Functions

The following functions are essential for programmers to manipulate strings.

Table 1: String Functions

Functions that take an action or update the string.

Function	Description
capitalize()	Capitalizes the initial character.
count()	Counts the numbers of a specified value in a string.
find()	Locates the position of a specified value in a string.
index()	Locates the position of a specified value in a string.
lower()	Converts the entire string to lowercase.
replace()	Replaces a specified value with another in the string.
swapcase()	Swaps the case of characters; lowercase becomes uppercase and vice versa.
title()	Capitalizes the first character of each word.
upper()	Converts the entire string to uppercase.
len()	Determines the length (number of characters) of the string.

Example 7B: Ignore Cases

In the previous code challenge, an issue arose when a user entered a country from the list with different case letters, resulting in not being found. In this updated example, we address this using the lower() function, which converts all user-input letters to lowercase. We also convert all country names on the list to lowercase. By doing so, we can effectively compare the user's input and country list in lowercase. This trick eliminates all the uppercase and compares two country names that contain only lowercase.

We will translate the above explanation into Python code.

find_country.py

```python
countries = "United States, United Kingdom, Germany, India,
Brazil, Spain, Italy, Canada, Japan, Mexico"
print("Current List: ", countries)
country = input("\nEnter a country name: ")


# convert the country entered by the user to lower case letters
country_lowercase = country.lower()
# convert the countries list to lower case letters
countries_lowercase = countries.lower()
# display the list and the user input in lower case
print("User input in lower case: ", country.lower())
print(countries.lower())


print("Is ", country, "on the list? ", country_lowercase in
countries_lowercase)
```

The user enters "GeRMany", which is on the list, but the program ignores the letter case and returns true this time.

```
Current List:  United States, United Kingdom, Germany, India, Brazil, Spain, Italy,
Canada, Japan, Mexico

Enter a country name: GeRMany
User input in lower case:  germany
united states, united kingdom, germany, india, brazil, spain, italy, canada, japan, mexico
Is  GeRMany on the list?  True
```

Example 8: Using String Functions

The following code example clarifies using the above string functions list.

string_functions.py

```python
text = "i am from Spain"

# prints I, converts the first "i" to capital I
print(text.capitalize())
# prints 2, the position of the first letter "a"
print(text.count("a"))
# prints 10, the position of the first letter of Spain in the
text
print(text.find("Spain"))
# prints 6, the position of the first r letter
print(text.index("r"))
# prints the text in lowercase
print(text.lower())
# replaces the country Spain with the US
print(text.replace("Spain", "US"))
# swaps all the letter cases of the text
print(text.swapcase())
# converts the first letter of the words to upper case
print(text.title())
# prints the length of the text, including the spaces
print(len(text))
```

Output

```
I am from spain
2
10
6
i am from spain
i am from US
I AM FROM sPAIN
I Am From Spain
15
```

Table 2: Functions Return True or False

String functions that return either true or false.

Function	Description
endswith()	Validates whether the string ends with a particular value.
isalnum()	Verifies if all characters in the string are alphanumeric.
isalpha()	Checks if all characters in the string belong to the alphabet.
isdigit()	Checks if all characters in the string are numeric.
islower()	Validates if all characters in the string are in lowercase.
isnumeric()	Verifies if all characters in the string are numeric.
istitle()	Checks if the string follows the title format rules.
isupper()	Validates if all characters in the string are in uppercase.
startswith()	Examines if the string initiates with a specific value.

Example 9: Boolean Functions

boolean_functions.py

```python
string1 = "Energy flows where attention goes"
string2 = "Tu1212HIJ"
string3 = "HiEveryBody"
string4 = "0137843626572"
string5 = "heis"
string6 = "8847463"
string7 = "Energy Flows Where Attention Goes"
string8 = "ENERGY FLOWS WHERE ATTENTION GOES"

# returns true because string1 starts with En
print(string1.startswith("En"))
# returns true because string1 ends with es
print(string1.endswith("es"))
# returns true because string2 contains only alphanumeric
print(string2.isalnum())
```

```python
# returns true because string3 contains only alphabet
print(string3.isalpha())
# returns true because string4 contains only numbers
print(string4.isdigit())
#  returns true, because string5 contains only lowercase letters
print(string5.islower())
#  returns true, because string6 contains only numbers
print(string6.isnumeric())
# returns true, because all the words in string7 starts with
uppercase
print(string7.istitle())
# returns true, because string8 contains only uppercase
print(string8.isupper())
```

Output

Notice

As a programmer, it is crucial to understand code and to have an expectation regarding the output. However, experts can see what the code does faster, but training yourself for that is essential; therefore, I offer quizzes in most of my books.

Quiz 1: Conversion

When executed, this code prompts the user to input the bread price, then the milk prices, and then calculates the total by summing both prices. Assuming the user enters prices of $2.50 for bread and $3.50 for milk, what will be the outcome of running this code?

calculator.py

```python
bread_price = input("Enter the price of bread: ")
milk_price = input("Enter the price of milk: ")

total_price = bread_price + milk_price
print(total_price)
```

Select the correct answer:

a. The code prints "6.0" to the output.

b. The code prints "2.503.50" to the output.

c. The code prints "6" to the output.

d. The code causes an error.

e. The code has no output.

Quiz 2: Conversion

Which shape do you expect to be created with the letter "X" in the output of the following program?

shape.py

```python
symbol = " X "
print(symbol * 10)
print(symbol * 10)
print(symbol * 10)
print(symbol * 10)
print(symbol * 10)
print(symbol * 10)
```

Select the correct answer:

a. The code prints a "triangle" to the output.

b. The code prints a "circle" to the output.

c. The code prints a "rectangle" to the output.

d. The code prints an "unknown shape" to the output.

e. The code causes an error.

f. The code has no output.

Quiz 3: String Manipulation

Which of the following statements converts the word 'price' in the code text to 'amount'?

The expected output of the program is: Python course amount: $2400

string_manipulation.py

```
text = "Python course price: $2400"
# insert the statement here
```

Select the correct answer:

a. The method print(text.replace('price', 'amount'))

b. The method print(text.convert('price', 'amount'))

c. The method print(text.change('price', 'amount'))

d. The method print(text.swap('price', 'amount'))

e. The method print(text.switch('price', 'amount'))

Quiz 4: String Index

What happens if the following code is run?

substring.py

```
title = "Python for beginners"

print(title[7])
```

Select the correct answer:

a. The code prints "7" to the output.

b. The code prints "f" to the output.

c. The code prints "n" to the output.

d. The code prints "o" to the output.

e. The code prints nothing to the output.

Exercise 1: String Index

Write a program that prints the following from this quote.

1. Print the word "journey" from the text using the position of the letters.
2. Print the word "journey" in uppercase using the function upper.
2. Print the whole quote in uppercase.
3. Print the number of the characters in the quote, including spaces.
4. Check whether the quote contains only alphanumeric using the function isalnum().

string_function.py

```python
quote = "A journey of a thousand miles begins with a single step"
# add your code
```

The expected output of the program is shown below.

```
journey
JOURNEY
A JOURNEY OF A THOUSAND MILES BEGINS WITH A SINGLE STEP
55
False
```

Exercise 2: Find Historical Figures

Write a program that allows users to enter the name of a historical figure. The program seeks the names in the list "Darwin, Einstein, Lincoln, Gandhi, Bonaparte, Tolstoy." If the name is on the list, the program returns true; otherwise, it is false, as shown in the outputs.

find.py

```
historical_figures = "Darwin, Einstein, Lincoln, Gandhi,
Bonaparte, Tolstoy"
# add your code
```

In the following output, the user enters LINCOLN.

```
Enter a name of a historical figure: LINCOLN
Is the name LINCOLN on the list?  True
```

In the following output, the user enters Newton.

```
Enter a name of a historical figure: Newton
Is the name Newton on the list?  False
```

Answers to the Exercises

Answer Quiz 1

As explained earlier, a user input is a string even if the user enters a number.

- If you join two strings with a "+" sign, the second string will be appended to the end of the first one.
- The prices are 2.50 and 3.50.
- Therefore, the answer is 2.503.50.
- The correct answer is b.

Output

```
Enter the price of bread: 2.50
Enter the price of milk: 3.50
2.503.50
```

Answer Quiz 2

When a string is multiplied by a number in Python, the string is replicated by that specified number. In the example, the character 'X' is multiplied by ten and subsequently printed. As a result, the character 'X' is printed ten times across six rows, forming a rectangular shape. Therefore, the correct answer is option c.

Output

```
X X X X X X X X X X
X X X X X X X X X X
X X X X X X X X X X
X X X X X X X X X X
X X X X X X X X X X
X X X X X X X X X X
```

Answer Quiz 3

As shown in the table of string functions, the function replace is used to replace a substring. In this case, the word "price" is replaced with the word "amount".

The correct answer is a.

Answer Quiz 4

- The title "Python for Beginners" contains 20 characters, including two spaces.
- The statement print(title[7]) prints the character in the seventh position, starting with the zero position. Therefore, it prints the letter "f" to the output, as shown below.

The correct answer is b.

0	1	2	3	4	5	6	7	8	9	10	11	12	13	14	15	16	17	18	19
P	y	t	h	o	n		f	o	r		B	e	g	i	n	n	e	r	s

Answer Exercise 1

Here below is the code required by the exercise.

string_functions.py

```python
quote = "A journey of a thousand miles begins with a single step"
# add your code
print(quote[2:9])
print(quote[2:9].upper())
print(quote.upper())
print(len(quote))
print(quote.isalnum())
```

Output

```
journey
JOURNEY
A JOURNEY OF A THOUSAND MILES BEGINS WITH A SINGLE STEP
55
False
```

Answer Exercise 2

find.py

```python
historical_figures = "Darwin, Einstein, Lincoln, Gandhi,
Bonaparte, Tolstoy"
# add your code
hf = input("Enter a name of a historical figure: ")
hf_ignore_case = hf.lower()
hf_list_ignor_case = historical_figures.lower()

print("Is the name", hf, "on the list? ", hf_ignore_case in
hf_list_ignor_case)
```

Output

```
Enter a name of a historical figure: EINSTEIN
Is the name EINSTEIN on the list?  True
```

5. Conditional Statements

So far, the statements of the previous programs were executed from the top to the bottom. Sometimes, we need only a statement executed if it meets a specific condition; otherwise, the program should ignore it.

For example, a particular shopping website offers a discount to subscribed customers, but an unsubscribed customer should pay the total price of a specific Item. In Python and other programming languages, conditional statements are used to determine whether a particular part of the code is executed or ignored.

Conditional statements are if statements, if else statements, and if elif statements.

If... Statements

If the condition meets specific requirements, the statements within the if-block are executed.

The if-block starts with if followed by the condition, then ends with a colon ":"

The if condition is followed by its block statements, which are recognized by a tab space, as shown in the code below.

```
if is_subscribed:      # the if condition
    price -= 5         # the if block
```

The statements within the if-block could be one or more statements. Once the if condition returns true, all the statements within the if-block are executed.

Example 1A: Discount Calculation

In the following example, if a customer subscribes, he receives a discount of $5. Otherwise, he doesn't. The boolean variable is_subscribed is false;

therefore, the statement if is_subscribed returns false, and the if-block is ignored.

The program prints the full price of $24.

The sep="" is added to the second print function to remove the space between the $ sign and the price.

discount.py

```python
price = 24
# the following customer is not subscribed
is_subscribed = False

if is_subscribed:        # the if condition
    price -= 5           # the if block


print("Price: $", price)
print('Price: $', price, sep="")
```

The output of the program

```
Price: $ 24
Price: $24
```

Example 1B: Discount Calculation

Let's set the value of the variable is_subscribed to true and execute the program again. This time, the if-statement returns true; therefore, the if-block is executed. The statement price -= 5 decreases the value of the price by 5. The output of the program is $19

discount.py

```python
price = 24
# the following customer is subscribed
is_subscribed = True

if is_subscribed:        # the if condition
    price -= 5           # the if block
'''

the statement sep="" to remove the space
between the $ sign and the price
```

```
'''
print('Price: $', price, sep="")
```

The output of the program

```
Price: $19
```

If...else Statements

If the condition meets specific requirements, the statements within the if block are executed. If the "if condition" returns false, you can tell Python to execute another block using the else statement shown in the following code.

Example 2A: Secret Number

Write a program that allows users to guess a secret number from 1 to 10. If the user's guess number is correct, the program confirms that the guess number is correct; otherwise, it is incorrect.

secret.py

```
secret_number = 8
guess_nr = input("Guess a number from (1 to 10): ")

# the guessnumber should be converted to a number
guess_nr = int(guess_nr)

if guess_nr == secret_number:
    print("Number", guess_nr, "is correct")
else:
    print("Number", guess_nr, "is incorrect")
```

Output 1: The user enters the number 5 in the following output.

```
Guess a number from (1 to 10): 5
Number 5 is incorrect
```

Output 2: The user enters the number 8 in the following output.

```
Guess a number from (1 to 10): 8
```

If-If... else Statements

If a conditional statement includes multiple if-statements, each statement that is evaluated to be true will be executed. The if-statements could be ended with an else-statement. The execution of the else statement depends on the outcome of the last if statement. If the final if-statement evaluates to true, the else-statement is ignored; however, if the last if-statement is false, the else-statement is executed.

Example 3A: Wage

A company pays the employee a basic salary of $3200 plus a combination of extra if he meets the following criteria.
- If he is certified, he receives a monthly extra amount of $200.
- If he is 40 years or older, he gets an extra $500.
- If he has four or more years of experience, he receives an extra $600.

In this example, the employee receives a basic wage of $3200. The boolean variable is_certified is True. Therefore, he gets an extra amount of $200. The employee in our example has four years of experience. Consequently, he receives an additional amount of $500. He is 43 years old and gets an extra $600. If you run the following program, the total wage of the employee

wage.py

```
basic_wage = 3200
is_certified = True
years_experience = 4
age = 43
total_wage = basic_wage
```

```python
if is_certified:
    total_wage  += 200
if years_experience >= 4:
    total_wage += 500
if age >= 40:
    total_wage += 600


print("Total wage: $",total_wage, sep='')
```

Output: If you run the program, the output below is shown.

```
Total wage: $4500
```

Example 3B: Wage

Change the variable values of the previous example as shown below. What is your expected output of the following program?

The basic wage is still $3200; the programmer is not certified; therefore, he will not receive the extra $200. However, he gets the additional $500 because he has five years of experience. He is 34 years old; therefore, he doesn't receive the extra $500 because he is under 40. His salary would be 3200 + 500 = 3700.

wage.py

```python
basic_wage = 3200
is_certified = True
years_experience = 4
age = 43
total_wage = basic_wage


if is_certified:
    total_wage  += 200
if years_experience >= 4:
```

```python
    total_wage += 500
if age >= 40:
    total_wage += 600

print("Total wage: $",total_wage, sep='')
```

The output of the program is shown below.

```
Total wage: $3700
```

If-elif... else Statements

By working with if-elif statements, the program starts with the first if statement. If the first if is evaluated as true, the block associated with it is executed, and the rest of the elif statements are ignored.

However, if the first if statement returns false, the program goes further with the following elif statement. If the next elif is evaluated as true, its block code is executed, and the rest of the elif statements are ignored.

By the series of if-elif statements, only the first statement that returns true is executed.

Example 3C: Wage

We use the previous example code but change the if-statement to elif statements. In the following code, the employee is certified, so the first if-statement returns true. Therefore, the if-block is executed, and the employee receives an extra $200 above the basic salary.

As shown in the code, the employee has five years of experience, but the rest of the code is ignored. That is because, by the elif statement, only the first statement that returns true is executed.

wage.py

```python
basic_wage = 3200
is_certified = True
years_experience = 5
age = 34
total_wage = basic_wage
if is_certified:
    total_wage  += 200
elif years_experience >= 4:
    total_wage += 500
elif age >= 40:
    total_wage += 600


print("Total wage: $",total_wage, sep='')
```

The output of the program is shown below.

```
Total wage: $3400
```

Quiz 1: Car Price

What happens if the following code is run?

car_price.py

```python
price_car = 9500
is_customer = True
age = 50

if is_customer:
    price_car -= 500
if age > 50:
    price_car -= 200

print(price_car)
```

Select the correct answer:

a. The code prints "9000" to the output.

b. The code prints "8800" to the output.

c. The code prints "9500" to the output.

d. The code prints "500" to the output.

e. The code prints nothing to the output.

Quiz 2: Car Price

What happens if the following code is run?

car_price.py

```python
price_car = 9500
is_customer = True
age = 55

if age > 50:
    price_car -= 200
elif is_customer:
    price_car -= 300

print(price_car)
```

Select the correct answer:

a. The code prints "9500" to the output.

b. The code prints "9300" to the output.

c. The code prints "9000" to the output.

d. The code prints "9200" to the output.

e. The code prints nothing to the output.

Quiz 3: If Statements

What happens if the following code is run?

if_else.py

```python
grade = 6
display = ""

if grade == 6:
    display += "X "
if grade > 5:
    display += "N "
if grade > 9:
    display += "P "
else:
    display += "K "

print(display)
```

Select the correct answer:

a. The code prints "X N" to the output.

b. The code prints "X " to the output.

c. The code prints "X K" to the output.

d. The code prints "X N K " to the output.

e. The code prints nothing to the output.

Quiz 4: If Elif Statements

What happens if the following code is run?

if_elif.py

```python
grade = 6
display = ""

if grade == 5:
    display += "X "
elif grade > 5:
    display += "N "
elif grade == 6:
    display += "P "
else:
```

```
    display += "K "

print(display)
```

Select the correct answer:

a. The code prints "X K" to the output.

b. The code prints "N K " to the output.

c. The code prints "N " to the output.

d. The code prints "N P " to the output.

e. The code prints nothing to the output.

Quiz 5: If Elif Statements

What happens if the following code is run?

if_elif.py

```python
grade = 3
display = ""

if grade == 5:
    display += "X "
elif grade > 5:
    display += "N "
elif grade == 6:
    display += "P "
else:
    display += "K "

print(display)
```

Select the correct answer:

a. The code prints "X K" to the output.

b. The code prints "K " to the output.

c. The code prints "X N " to the output.

d. The code prints "N K " to the output.

e. The code prints nothing to the output.

Quiz 6: Logical Operator

What happens if the following code is run?

laptop.py

```python
ram = 16
harddisk = 150
screen = 17
price = 600

if ram >= 16 and harddisk >= 200:
    price += 200
if ram >= 16 or harddisk >= 200:
    price += 100
if ram >= 8 and harddisk >= 100 and screen >= 20:
    price += 150
else:
    price -= 150

print(price)
```

Select the correct answer:

a. The code prints "800" to the output.

b. The code prints "900" to the output.

c. The code prints "550" to the output.

d. The code prints "700" to the output.

e. The code prints nothing to the output.

Quiz 7: Logical Operator

What happens if the following code is run?

laptop.py

```python
ram = 16
harddisk = 150
screen = 17
price = 600

if ram >= 16 and harddisk >= 150:
    price += 200
elif ram >= 16 or harddisk >= 200:
    price += 100
elif ram >= 8 and harddisk >= 100 and screen >= 17:
    price += 150
else:
    price -= 150

print(price)
```

Select the correct answer:

a. The code prints "800" to the output.

b. The code prints "900" to the output.

c. The code prints "550" to the output.

d. The code prints "700" to the output.

e. The code prints nothing to the output.

Exercise 1: Convert Euro to Dollars

Create a program that enables users to enter a specified amount in Euros, and the program should then convert this amount into dollars, considering the exchange rate of 1 Euro is equivalent to $1.10.

Output 1: The user enters an amount of 100 euro

```
Enter an amount in Euros: 100
The amount of 100.0 is $110.00
```

Output 2: The user enters an amount of 120 euro

```
Enter an amount in Euros: 120
The amount of 120.0 is $132.00
```

Exercise 2: Volleyball Team

A volleyball team is actively seeking young players to join their team. To be eligible, a player must meet the following criteria:
- Height: 185 cm (72.9 inches) or taller.
- Age: Between 18 and 25 years old.
- Experience: A minimum of two years in the field.

The program selects players meeting these requirements. Otherwise, they are rejected.

volleyball.py

```python
height = input("Enter the height of the player: ")
# convert the height to an integer
height = int(height)


# add your code
```

The expected output of the program is shown below. The user enters a height of 185 cm, an age of 19 years, and an experience of 2 years. The program selects the player.

```
Enter the height of the player: 185
Enter the age of the player: 19
Enter years of experience: 2
The player is accepted.
```

The expected output of the program is shown below. The user enters a height of 188 cm, an age of 26 years, and an experience of 3 years. The program rejects the player because his age doesn't meet the requirements.

```
Enter the height of the player: 188
Enter the age of the player: 26
Enter years of experience: 3
The player is rejected.
```

Answers to the Exercises

Answer Quiz 1

- The first if statement checks if the variable is_customer is true, which is true as it is initialized as true.
- The block is executed, and the statement price_car -= 500 decreases the value of the car price by $500. The price of the car becomes 9500 - 500 = 9000.
- The second if statement checks whether the customer's age is greater than 50, which is not because the customer is 50; therefore, the block is ignored.
- The first statement decreased the price of the car by 500. Therefore, the car's price becomes 9000.

The correct answer is a.

Output

```
9000
```

Answer Quiz 2

- The first if-statement checks whether the customer is older than 50 years, which is true because the customer is 55.
- The block is executed, and the price of the car is decreased by $200.
- 9500 - 200 = 9300.
- The second elif statement checks whether the variable customer is set to true, which is true. However, the block is not executed because by the elif statement, only the first statement that returns true is executed, and the rest of the conditions are ignored.

The correct answer is b.

Output

```
9300
```

Answer Quiz 3

The variable display is an empty string.

- The first if-statement checks whether the grade is equal to six, which is correct. Therefore, its body is executed, and the letter "X" is appended to the display variable.
- The second if-statement checks whether the grade is larger than five, which is true. Therefore, the "N" is also appended to the display variable.
- The third if-statement checks whether the grade is larger than nine, which is not true; therefore, the block is ignored.
- The last if-statement returns false; therefore, the else statement is executed, and the letter "K" is appended to the display variable.
- The value of the display variable becomes "X N K."

The correct answer is d.

Output

```
X N K
```

Answer Quiz 4

- The first if-statement checks whether the grade is equal to five, which is false. Therefore, the block is ignored.
- The second elif-statement checks whether the grade is larger than five, which is true. The block is executed, and the value "N" is added to the variable display.
- By elif-statements, all the rest of the statements are ignored when the

first true condition is found.

The correct answer is c.

Output

```
N
```

Answer Quiz 5

- The first if-statement checks whether the grade is equal to five, which is false.
- The second elif-statement checks whether the grade is larger than five, which is false.
- The third elif-statement checks whether the grade is equal to six, which is false.
- All the elif-statements were false; therefore, the else statement is executed and adds the letter "K" to the value of the display variable.

The correct answer is b.

Output

```
K
```

Answer Quiz 6

- The first if-statement checks whether the RAM is equal to or larger than 16, which returns true, but the hard disk is not equal to or larger than 200. Therefore, the block is ignored by logical operation because all the operands must return true; otherwise, the condition returns false.
- The second if-statement returns true because by the logical operator "or," the statement returns true if one operand is true. In this case, the ram is equal to or larger than 16. The price is incremented by 100.
- For the third if-statement, the logical operator "and" is used. The last operand checks whether the screen is equal to or larger than 20,

which is false. Therefore, the whole conditional statement returns false.

- The else-statement is executed because the last if-statement returns false. The price is decreased by 150.
- The price = 600 + 100 - 150 = 550

The correct answer is c.

Output

```
550
```

Answer Quiz 7

- The first if-statement checks whether the ram is equal to or larger than 16, which returns true; the hard disk is also equal to or larger than 150, which is true. Therefore, the block is executed, and the price is incremented by 200 and becomes 800.
- By elif-statements, the rest of the statements are ignored when the first true condition is reached.

The correct answer is a.

Output

```
800
```

Answer Exercise 1

currency.py

```python
amount_euro = input("Enter an amount in Euros: ")
# convert the euro amount to float
amount_euro = float(amount_euro)


amount_dollar = amount_euro * 1.10
print("The amount of",amount_euro, "is $%.2f" %amount_dollar)
```

Output

```
Enter an amount in Euros: 200
The amount of 200.0 is $220.00
```

Answer Exercise 2

volleyball.py

```python
height = input("Enter the height of the player: ")
# convert the height to an integer
height = int(height)
age = input("Enter the age of the player: ")
# convert the age to an integer
age = int(age)
experience = input("Enter years of experience: ")
# convert the experience to an integer
experience = int(experience)

if height >= 185 and age >= 18 and age <= 25 and experience >= 2:
    print("The player is accepted.")
else:
    print("The player is rejected. ")
```

Output

```
Enter the height of the player: 190
Enter the age of the player: 24
Enter years of experience: 1
The player is rejected.
```

6. Loops Statements

A loop controls the repetition of a specific statement(s) by determining the number of times executed. A loop contains a head and a body, with the head specifying the frequency of statement execution within the loop's body. In Python, the loop's body is positioned beneath the head and should be indented with a "tab" to the right, as shown in the code below.

The While Loop

A while loop iterates through the execution of its body as long as the specified condition evaluates as true.

Example 1: While Loop

The following code illustrates the while loop.

```python
nr = 1
while nr < 5:                               # head of the loop
    print(nr, 'is smaller than 5') # body: statement 1
    nr += 1                                 # body: statement 2


print("number is: ", nr)    # doesn't belong to the loop
```

The value "1" is assigned to the variable "nr" in the example. The body is executed as long as the while condition returns true.
- The initial value of the variable nr is 1. The head of the loop checks whether the value 1 is smaller than 5, and it is. Therefore, the loop's head condition returns true.
- The body's statements of the while-loop are executed, and print "1 is smaller than 5."
- The statement "nr += 1" increments the value of the variable nr by one. Therefore, the value of nr becomes 2.

- The program returns to the head and checks whether the value 2 is smaller than 5. The answer is true; therefore, the loop's body is executed, and the statement "2 is smaller than 5" is printed.
- When the value of variable nr reaches "5", the head of the loop checks whether "5" is smaller than "5," and that returns false because it is not. Therefore, the execution of the loop's body is terminated.

The output of the program is.

```
1 is smaller than 5
2 is smaller than 5
3 is smaller than 5
4 is smaller than 5
number is:  5
```

The While True statement

The statement "while True" is used in Python to execute one or more statements continuously.

Example 2: The While True Statement

The following program prints "How old are you?" repeatedly because the while true statement returns always true.

```python
while True:
    print("How old are you?")
```

Here is the output of the program.

```
....
How old are you?
How old are you?
How old are you?
How old are you?
How old are you?
How old are you?
How old are you?
How old are you?
continues.............
```

The Break keyword

The break statement is used to terminate a loop.

Example 3: The Break Statement

If you run the following example, the statement "How old are you?" is printed once. As soon as the break statement is reached, the loop is terminated.

```python
while True:
    print("How old are you?")
    break
```

The output of the code.

```
How old are you?
```

The Continue keyword

The continue keyword skips the current iteration in a loop and continues to the next iteration.

Example 4: The Continue Statement

If you run the following code, the value of the variable nr is printed. If the value of the variable nr is reached 4, 6, and 8, the statement "continue" skips those numbers, as shown below.

```python
nr = 0
while nr < 10:
    nr += 1
    if(nr == 4 or nr == 6 or nr == 8):
        continue    # skip
    print(nr)
```

The output of the code.

```
1
```

```
2
3
5
7
9
10
```

The Pass keyword

In conditional statements and loops, the body of the loop or the body of the conditional statement cannot be left empty. The pass statement ensures the code doesn't generate an error and allows the programmer to write the required code later.

Example 5: The Pass Statement

If you run the following example, the statement "pass" ensures that Python doesn't mention an error. In that way programmers can later change the pass to any statements they wish.

```python
nr = 0
while nr < 5:
    if nr == 3:
        print(nr)
    else:
        pass
    nr += 1
```

The output of the code.

```
3
```

The For Loop

The range() function in Python determines how often a for-loop is executed based on specific values. You can pass one, two, or three parameters to the range function. The value of the one-parameter determines when the loop must stop.

Passing One Parameter to range(stop)

Example	Description
range(9)	Starts by default with 0, ends with 8 (9 is not included), and the start by default increments by one. So, the reeks numbers are 0, 1, 2, 3, 4, 5, 6, 7, 8.
range(4)	starts by default with 0, ends with 3 (4 is not included), and the start by default increments by one. So, the reeks numbers are: 0, 1, 2, 3.

Example 6: Range Function With One Parameter

In the following code, only one parameter, 4, is passed to the function range().

```
for number in range(4):
    print(number)
```

The output of the code.

Passing Two Parameter to range(start, stop)

By passing two parameters through the function range(start, stop),

- The first parameter is the "start" or the initial value of the variable
- The second parameter is the value where the loop should stop.
- The start value is incremented each time by one by default.

Example	Description
range(3, 7)	It starts with 3, ends with 6 (7 is not included), and the start each time by default increments by one. So, the reeks numbers are: 3, 4, 5, 6.
range(5, 8)	It starts with 5, ends with 7 (8 is not included), and the start by default increments by one. So, the reeks numbers are: 5, 6, 7.

Example 7: Range Function With Two Parameter

The code of the following example prints
- From the start, which is 5.
- To the stop, which is 9 (9 is not included).
- By default, the start value increments by one.

```python
for number in range(5, 9):
    print(number)
```

The output of the program is.

```
5
6
7
8
```

Passing Three Parameter to range(start, stop, increment)

By passing three parameters through the function range(start, stop, increment)
- The first parameter is the "start" or the initial value of the variable
- The second parameter is the value where the loop should stop.
- The third parameter's value determines with which number each time the variable starts is incremented.

Examples	Description

range(3, 10, 2)   Starts with 3, ends with 9 (10 is not included), and the start each time is incremented by 2. So, the reeks numbers are: 3, 5, 7, 9.

range(2, 11, 3)   Starts with two and ends with 10 (11 is not included), and the start each time is incremented by 3. So, the reeks numbers are: 2, 5, 8. The end number is eight because if we increment eight by 3, we reach 11, which is not included.

Example 8: Range With 3 Parameters

If the following code is run, the output is 2, 5, 8.

```python
for number in range(2, 11, 3):
    print(number)
```

The output of the code.

```
2
5
8
```

Quiz 1: While Loop

What happens if the following code is run?

while_loop.py

```python
id = 6

while id < 10:
    print(id, end=' ')  # statement 1
    id += 1             # statement 2
```

Select the correct answer:

a. The code prints "1 2 3 4 " to the output.

b. The code prints "10 " to the output.

c. The code prints "6 7 8 9 " to the output.

d. The code prints "6 7 8 " to the output.

e. The code prints nothing to the output.

Quiz 2: While Loop

We remove statement 2 from the previous example and rerun the code.
What happens if the following code is run?

while_loop.py

```python
id = 6

while id < 10:
    print(id, end=' ') # statement 1
```

Select the correct answer:

a. The code prints "1 2 3 4 " to the output.

b. The code prints "6 7 8 9 " to the output.

c. The code prints "6 7 8 9 10" to the output.

d. The code continually prints 6 to the output.

e. The code prints nothing to the output.

Quiz 3: Break Statement

What happens if the following code is run?

break_statement.py

```python
nr = 2
while True:
    nr += 1
    print(nr, end=' ')
```

```python
if nr >= 5:
    break
```

Select the correct answer:

a. The code prints "2 3 4 5 " to the output.

b. The code prints "3 4 5 " to the output.

c. The code prints "2 3 4 " to the output.

d. The code prints "2 3 " to the output.

e. The code prints nothing to the output.

Quiz 4: Continue Statements

What happens if the following code is run?

continue_statement.py

```python
nr = 1
while nr < 6:
    nr += 1
    # if the rest = 0 as a result of dividing the nr by 2.
    if nr % 2 == 0:
        continue
    else:
        print(nr, end=' ')
```

Select the correct answer:

a. The code prints "1 2 3 4 5 6 " to the output.

b. The code prints "3 4 5 " to the output.

c. The code prints "3 5 " to the output.

d. The code prints "2 3 " to the output.

e. The code prints nothing to the output.

Quiz 5: Pass Statements

What happens if the following code is run?

pass.py

```python
nr = 0
while nr < 10:
    if nr >= 5 or nr < 3:
        pass
    else:
        print(nr, end = ' ')
    nr += 1
```

Select the correct answer:

a. The code prints "0 1 2 3 4 5 " to the output.

b. The code prints "3 4 5 " to the output.

c. The code prints "3 4 " to the output.

d. The code prints "2 3 4 " to the output.

e. The code prints nothing to the output.

Quiz 6: For Loop Range One Parameter

What happens if the following code is run?

for_loop.py

```python
for number in range (5):
    print(number, end = ' ')
```

Select the correct answer:

a. The code prints "0 1 2 3 " to the output.

b. The code prints "0 1 2 " to the output.

c. The code prints "0 1 2 3 4 " to the output.

d. The code prints "0 1 2 3 4 5 " to the output.

e. The code prints nothing to the output.

Quiz 7: For Loop Range Two Parameter

What happens if the following code is run?

range_2param.py

```python
for number in range (8, 10):
    print(number, end = ' ')
```

Select the correct answer:

a. The code prints "8 9 10 " to the output.

b. The code prints "0 1 2 3 4 5 6 7 8 9 " to the output.

c. The code prints "7 8 9 " to the output.

d. The code prints "8 9 " to the output.

e. The code prints nothing to the output.

Quiz 8: For Loop Range Three Parameter

What happens if the following code is run?

range_3param.py

```python
for number in range (2, 10, 7):
    print(number, end = ' ')
```

Select the correct answer:

a. The code prints "2 3 4 5 6" to the output.

b. The code prints "2 3 4 5 6 7 8 9 " to the output.

c. The code prints "2 3 4 5 6 7 " to the output.

d. The code prints "2 9 " to the output.

e. The code prints nothing to the output.

Exercise 1: While Loop

The following program prints the numbers from 1 to 10. Add a combination of if-statement and a continue-statement to skip 5, 6, and 7.

while_loop.py

```python
nr = 0

while nr < 10:
    nr += 1
    # add your code here
    print(nr, end=", ")
```

Current output

```
1, 2, 3, 4, 5, 6, 7, 8, 9, 10,
```

The expected output after adding your code

```
1, 2, 3, 4, 8, 9, 10,
```

Exercise 2: For Loop

Update the following program by changing the values of the three zero parameters of the numbers in the range function to print the output "10, 13, 16, 19", as shown below.

for_loop.py

```python
# change the parameters of the range function to achieve the
result
for number in range(0, 0, 0):
    print(number, end=' ')
```

The expected output

```
10 13 16 19
```

Answers to the Exercises

Answer Quiz 1

- The initial value of the variable id is 6.
- The statement "while id < 10" means as long as "id" is smaller than 10, the body of the loop must be executed.
- The statement 1 prints the initial value of id, which is 6.
- Statement 2 increments the value of id by one.
- The value of id becomes 7. The while loop checks whether seven is smaller than ten, which is. Therefore, 7 is printed to the output.
- The previous repetition continues until the value of id becomes 10. In that case, 10 is not smaller than 10; therefore, the loop is terminated.

The correct answer is c.

Output

```
6 7 8 9
```

Answer Quiz 2

- The initial value of the variable id is 6.
- The statement "while id < 10" checks whether the value of id is smaller than 10, which is smaller. Therefore, the value 6 is printed to the output.
- The next time, the value 6 hasn't changed; therefore, 6 is printed again to the output.
- Since the value 6 doesn't change, printing 6 to the output continues.
- The program doesn't stop with printing 6 to the output because the while loop repeatedly checks whether 6 is smaller than 10, and it is.

The correct answer is d.

Output

```
6666666666666666666666666666666666666666666666666666
6666666666666666666666666666666666666666666666666666
6666666666666666666666666666666666666666666666666666
6666666666666666666666666666666666666666666666666666
6666666666666666666666666666666666666666666666666666
6666666666666666666666666666666666666666666666666666
6666666666666666666666666666666666666666666666666666
6666666666666666666666666666666666666666666666666666
6666666666666666666666666666666666666666666666666666
6666666666666666666666666666666666666666666666666666
6666666666666666666666666666666666666666666666666666
6666666666666666666666666666666666666666666666666666
6666666666666666666666666666666666666666666666666666
6666666666666666666666666666666666666666666666666666
6666666666666666666666666666666666666666666666666666
```

Answer Quiz 3

- The initial value of the variable nr is 2.
- The "while True" statement returns always true as long as there is no statement that stops it.
- The statement nr+= 1 increments the value of the nr variable by one, its value becomes 3, and it is printed to the output.
- The number is printed until it reaches 5.
- The statement if nr >= 5 checks whether the number is larger or equal to 5. Then, the break statement terminates the loop.

The correct answer is b.

Output

```
3 4 5
```

Answer Quiz 4

- The initial value of the variable nr is 1.

- The statement "while nr < 6" returns true because the value of nr is 1.
- The statement "nr+=1" increments the value of nr by one, and its value becomes 2.
- The statement "if nr % 2 == 0" checks whether the value of nr divided by two doesn't have a remainder. In that case, the continue statement skips it. Therefore, the values 2 and 4 are skipped because if you divide 2 or 4 by 2, the remainder is zero.
- The code prints 3 5 to the standard output.

The correct answer is c.

Output

```
3 5
```

Answer Quiz 5

- The initial value of the variable nr is 0.
- The statement "while nr < 10" checks whether the nr, which is 0, is smaller than 10, and it is.
- The statement "if nr >= 5 or nr < 3" checks the nr values if it is smaller than 3 and the numbers equal or larger than 5.
- In other cases, the value of the nr is printed to the output.

The correct answer is c.

Output

```
3 4
```

Answer Quiz 6

- The for loop in range (5) repeats the execution of the loop's body from 0 to 4. Remember that 5 is exclusive, and the start is 0 by default.

The correct answer is c.

Output

```
0 1 2 3 4
```

Answer Quiz 7

- The for loop range (8, 10) starts with 8 and stops at 10.
- The range includes 8 and 9.

The correct answer is d.

Output

```
8 9
```

Answer Quiz 8

- The for loop range (2, 10, 7) starts with 2 stops at 10 and increments the value by 7 each time.
- The range numbers are 2 and 9, and it stops there because otherwise, it exceeds the value of 10.

The correct answer is d.

Output

```
2 9
```

Answer Exercise 1

while_loop.py

```python
nr = 0

while nr < 10:
    nr += 1
    if(nr > 4 and nr < 8):
        continue
    print(nr, end=", ")
```

Output

```
1, 2, 3, 4, 8, 9, 10,
```

Answer Exercise 2

while_loop.py

```python
for number in range(10, 20, 3):
    print(number, end=' ')
```

Output

```
10 13 16 19
```

7. Lists in Python

A list is a data structure that stores multiple elements. In the real world, we often need lists of similar objects, for example, a list of cars, a list of students, a list of computers, and a list of items.

Python allows the creation of a list, as shown in the code below. By declaring a list, you have to choose an appropriate name for the list.
In the following example, we have declared a list to store cars; therefore, we call the list cars. Brackets enclose elements of a list in Python.

Example 1A: Declaring and Displaying a List

It is clear in the following example that each element inside the list has an index position. The index of the brand Volvo, for example, is 2.
The position of an element inside a list is indexed from 0.

0	1	2	3	4
Audi	**Tesla**	**Volvo**	**BMW**	**Toyota**

Declaring a List

In Python, you can create a list by following the next steps.
- Choose an appropriate name for the list; in this case, the name cars is appropriate.
- Open a bracket and start with the elements you want in the list.
- Separate the element's names with a comma.

Displaying Elements of a List Individually

Displaying starts with the print function.
- The name of the list ended with open and closed brackets.
- Pass the index of the element to the bracket.

Use the name of the list and the index of "1" to print the brand Tesla in the list, as shown below.

print(cars[1])

Example 1A: Displaying a List Element

The following example shows how to display elements of a list individually.

cars.py

```
# declare a list
cars = ["Audi", "Tesla", "Volvo", "BMW", "Toyota"]

# display elements of the list
print(cars[0])   # prints Audi
print(cars[1])   # prints Tesla
print(cars[2])   # prints Volvo
print(cars[3])   # prints BMW
print(cars[4])   # prints Toyota
```

The output of the previous code is.

```
Audi
Tesla
Volvo
BMW
Toyota
```

Displaying All The Elements of a List

If you have a massive number of elements on the list, displaying them individually would take a lot of time and a lot of lines of code. Sometimes, it is better to display list elements using a loop, as shown in the following example.

Example 1B: Displaying All the List Elements

In the following code, we use a loop to display all the list elements.

cars.py

```python
# declare a list
cars = ["Audi", "Tesla", "Volvo", "BMW", "Toyota"]

# display all the list elements
for element in cars:
    print(element)
```

The output of the code is the same as the previous example.

```
Audi
Tesla
Volvo
BMW
Toyota
```

List Modification

In the real world, a list doesn't remain the same. For example, a list of students. Some students could leave the university, and some students could join later. Think about how a student's address or other data can be changed in the future. Therefore, it is necessary to have functions that allow adding, removing, and updating list elements. We need even more functions to know how many elements are in the list or how to sort the elements of a list alphabetically..etc.

Table 1: Adding Elements to a List

Function	Description
Adding elements	

append()	Adds an element at the end of the list
insert()	Adds an element at the specified position
extend()	Add the elements of a list to the end of the current list

Table 2: Removing Elements From a List

Function	Description
Removing elements	
pop()	Removes the element at the specified position
remove()	Removes the first item with the specified value
clear()	Removes all the elements from the list

Table 3: Other List Functions

Function	Description
Other list functions	
len()	Returns the number of elements of the list
copy()	Returns a copy of the list
count()	Returns the number of elements with the specified value
index()	Returns the index of the first element with the specified value
reverse()	Reverses the order of the list
sort()	Sorts the list

Adding Elements to a List

We use the available functions such as append, insert, and extend to add elements to the list "cars."

Example 2: Add an Element to the End

We use the function append to add an element to the last position or the end of the list.

cars.py

```python
# declare a list
cars = ["Audi", "Tesla", "Volvo", "BMW", "Toyota"]

# append() adds an element at the end of the list
cars.append("Cadillac")

# display all the elements of the list
for element in cars:
    print(element, end = ' ')
```

The output clearly shows that Cadillac is added to the end of the list.

```
Audi Tesla Volvo BMW Toyota Cadillac
```

Example 3: Add an Element to a Specific Position

We use the function insert to add an element to a specific position of a list. We also specify the index where the new element should be placed.

cars.py

```python
# declare a list
cars = ["Audi", "Tesla", "Volvo", "BMW", "Toyota"]

# add  "Jaguar" at the fourth position in the list
cars.insert(3, "Jaguar")

# display all the elements of the list
for element in cars:
    print(element, end = ' ')
```

In the ouput we see clearly that the brand Jaguar is added to the third position or the index position 3 of the list.

```
Audi Tesla Volvo Jaguar BMW Toyota
```

Example 4: Add a List Element to a List

We can concatenate all list elements to another one using the extend function. In the following example, we add the elements of the sports cars list to the cars list using the function extend.

cars.py

```python
'''
merging two lists
'''

# declare a list
cars = ["Audi", "Tesla", "Volvo", "BMW", "Toyota"]


sport_cars = ["Aston Martin", "Ferrari", "Bugatti"]
# function extend() Adds the sport cars list
# to the end of the list cars
cars.extend(sport_cars)


# display all the elements of the list
for element in cars:
    print(element, end=' ')
```

The output of the code shows that the sport cars are added to the list cars.

```
Audi Tesla Volvo BMW Toyota Aston Martin Ferrari Bugatti
```

Removing Elements From a List

The following examples show how to remove elements from a list using the pop, remove, and clear functions.

Example 5: Removing Elements

We use the function remove to remove the element "Volvo" from the list.

cars.py

```python
# declare a list
cars = ["Audi", "Tesla", "Volvo", "BMW", "Toyota"]
# remove the element "Volvo" from the list
cars.remove("Volvo")

# display all the elements of the list
for element in cars:
    print(element, end=' ')
```

The output of the code shows that the element Volvo is removed from the list.

```
Audi Tesla BMW Toyota
```

Example 6: Removing Elements by Its Position

We use the function pop to remove the element on the index position "3". As shown in the code below, the brand "BMW" is in the third position, starting with zero.

cars.py

```python
# declare a list
cars = ["Audi", "Tesla", "Volvo", "BMW", "Toyota"]
# remove the element "BMW" from the list
cars.pop(3)

# display all the elements of the list
for element in cars:
    print(element, end=' ')
```

The output of the code shows that the element BMW is removed from the list.

```
Audi Tesla Volvo Toyota
```

Example 7: Removing All the Elements

We use the function clear to remove all the elements of a list.

cars.py

```python
# declare a list
cars = ["Audi", "Tesla", "Volvo", "BMW", "Toyota"]
# the clear function removes all the elements of the list
cars.clear()

# display all the elements of the list
for element in cars:
    print(element, end=' ')
```

The output of the code shows nothing because the function clear has removed all the cars from the list.

Example 8: Number of Elements

We use the function len to determine how many elements are on the list.

cars.py

```python
# declare a list
cars = ["Audi", "Tesla", "Volvo", "BMW", "Toyota"]

# the number elements of the cars list
nr_elements = len(cars)


print(nr_elements)
```

The output of the code shows that the number of the elements is "5".

Example 9: Sort Alphabetically

We use the function sort to sort elements of a list alphabetically, and the function reverse is used to reverse the sort.

cars.py

```python
# declare a list
cars = ["Audi", "Tesla", "Volvo", "BMW", "Toyota"]

cars.sort()
print("\n-----sorted alphabetically-------")
for element in cars:
    print(element, end=' ')

print("\n\n-----reverse-------")
cars.reverse()
# display all the cars
for element in cars:
    print(element, end=' ')
```

The output of the code.

```
-----sorted alphabetically-------
Audi BMW Tesla Toyota Volvo

-----reverse-------
Volvo Toyota Tesla BMW Audi
```

Example 10: List Copy

We use the function copy to copy a list. In the following example, we created a copy of the list of cars and sorted them alphabetically.

cars.py

```python
# declare a list
cars = ["Audi", "Tesla", "Volvo", "BMW", "Toyota"]
# copy() returns a copy of the list
```

```python
cars_copy = cars.copy()
cars_copy.sort()
# display all the elements of cars list
for element in cars:
    print(element)
print("----------")
# display all the elements of the cars copy list
# sorted alphabetically
for element in cars_copy:
    print(element)
```

The output of the code.

```
Audi
Tesla
Volvo
BMW
Toyota
----------
Audi
BMW
Tesla
Toyota
Volvo
```

Example 11: Numbers of a Specific Element

We use the function count to return the number of a specific element in the list.

cars.py

```python
# declare a list
cars = ["Audi", "Toyota", "Tesla", "Audi", "Volvo", "BMW",
"Audi", "Toyota"]
# returns the number of Audi elements
print(cars.count("Audi"))
# returns the number of Tesla elements
print(cars.count("Tesla"))
# returns the number of Toyota elements
print(cars.count("Toyota"))
```

The output of the code.

```
3
1
2
```

Example 12: Position of an Element

We use the function index to find the position of a specific element.

cars.py

```python
# declare a list
cars = ["Audi", "Tesla", "Volvo", "BMW", "Toyota"]
# find out the index position of Tesla
index_element = cars.index("Tesla")
# the index position of Tesla is one
print(index_element)
```

The output is "1" because the Tesla brand is in the index position of 1.

```
1
```

Quiz 1: Display Freelancer

What happens if the following code is run?

freelancers.py

```python
freelancers = ["Edward", "Jeff", "Robert", "Daniel", "John"]

freelancers.sort()
print(freelancers[0])
```

Select the correct answer:

a. The code prints "Edward" to the output.

b. The code prints "John" to the output.

c. The code prints "Jeff" to the output.

d. The code prints "Daniel" to the output.

e. The code prints nothing to the output.

Quiz 2: Display Freelancers

What happens if the following code is run?

freelancers.py

```python
freelancers = ["Edward", "Jeff", "Robert", "John", "Daniel"]


i = 0
for element in freelancers:
    if i == 2 or i == 4:
        print(element, end = ' ')
    i += 1
```

Select the correct answer:

a. The code prints "Robert Daniel " to the output.

b. The code prints "Jeff John " to the output.

c. The code prints "Robert " to the output.

d. The code prints "Edward Daniel " to the output.

e. The code prints nothing to the output.

Quiz 3: Modifying Freelancers List

What happens if the following code is run?

freelancers.py

```python
freelancers = ["Edward", "Jeff", "Robert", "John", "Daniel"]

freelancers.pop(2)
freelancers.append("Emma")

for element in freelancers:
        print(element, end = ' ')
```

Select the correct answer:

a. The code prints "Edward Jeff John Daniel Emma " to the output.

b. The code prints "Emma Edward John Daniel " to the output.

c. The code prints "Edward Jeff John Daniel " to the output.

d. The code prints "Edward Jeff Robert John Daniel Emma " to the output.

e. The code prints nothing to the output.

Quiz 4: Modifying Freelancers List

What happens if the following code is run?

freelancers.py

```python
freelancers = ["Edward", "Jeff", "Robert", "John", "Daniel"]


freelancers.remove("Daniel")
freelancers.remove("Robert")
freelancers.remove("Jeff")
freelancers.remove("Edward")
freelancers.insert(0, "Emma")


for element in freelancers:
        print(element, end = ' ')
```

Select the correct answer:

a. The code prints "Emma John " to the output.

b. The code prints "Emma Edward Jeff Robert John Daniel " to the output.

c. The code prints "Edward Jeff Robert John Daniel Emma " to the output.

d. The code prints "Edward Jeff Robert John Daniel " to the output.

e. The code prints nothing to the output.

Quiz 5: Copy Freelancers List

What happens if the following code is run?

freelancers.py

```python
freelancers = ["Edward", "Jeff", "Robert", "John", "Daniel"]
```

```
freelancers2 = freelancers.copy()
freelancers2.sort()

print(freelancers2[1], freelancers[1])
```

Select the correct answer:

a. The code prints "Jeff Jeff" to the output.

b. The code prints "Edward Daniel" to the output.

c. The code prints "Edward Jeff" to the output.

d. The code prints "Daniel Edward" to the output.

e. The code prints nothing to the output.

Exercise 1: Modify Pet's List

Write a program that declares a list of pets with the following elements.

- Dog, Cat, Snake, Rabbit, Fish
- Remove "Snake" from the list by using the function pop.
- Remove the element "Fish" from the list using the remove function.
- Add the new element Lizard" at the end of the list element.

The expected output of the program is shown below.

```
['Dog', 'Cat', 'Rabbit', 'Lizard']
```

Exercise 2: Sort Pet's List

Write a program that declares a list of pets with the following elements.

- Dog, Cat, Snake, Rabbit, Fish.
- Sort the elements alphabetically using the function sort.
- Display the number of the elements by using the function len.

The expected output of the program is shown below.

```
Sorted alphabetically:  ['Cat', 'Dog', 'Fish', 'Rabbit', 'Snake']
Elements number:  5
```

Answers to the Exercises

Answer Quiz 1

- After sorting the list, the order is changed to ['Daniel', 'Edward', 'Jeff', 'John', 'Robert']
- The statement print(freelancers[0]) prints the first element which Daniel.

The correct answer is d.

Output

```
Daniel
```

Answer Quiz 2

- The for loop iterates through the elements of the loop.
- The if i == 2 or i == 4 selects the elements with the index 2 and 4, which are Robert and Daniel.

The correct answer is a.

Output

```
Robert Daniel
```

Answer Quiz 3

- The statement freelancers.pop(2) removes the freelancer Robert from the list, because his index is 2.
- The statement freelancers.append("Emma") adds Emma to the end of the list.
- The correct answer is a.

Output

```
Edward Jeff John Daniel Emma
```

Answer Quiz 4

- The statement freelancers.remove("Daniel") removes Daniel from the list.
- The remove statements removes also Robert, Jeff and Edward from the list.
- The statement freelancers.insert(0, "Emma") adds Emma to the first position of the list.

The correct answer is a.

Output

```
Emma John
```

Answer Quiz 5

- The statement freelancers2 = freelancer.copy(), copies the list freelancers.
- The statement freelancers2.sort() sorts the freelancers2 list alphabetically.
- The statement print(freelancers2[1], freelancers[1]) the freelancers2 list is sorted alphabetically. Therefore, the name Edward is the at the index postion 1.\
- The freelancers is not sorted; therefore, the first index position is Jeff.

The correct answer is a.

Output

```
Edward Jeff
```

Answer Exercise 1

petslist.py

```python
pets = ["Dog", "Cat", "Snake", "Rabbit", "Fish"]

pets.pop(2)
pets.remove("Fish")
pets.append("Lizard")

print(pets)
```

Output

```
['Dog', 'Cat', 'Rabbit', 'Lizard']
```

Answer Exercise 2

petslist.py

```python
pets = ["Dog", "Cat", "Snake", "Rabbit", "Fish"]
pets.sort()

print("Sorted alphabetically: ", pets)
print("Elements number: ", len(pets))
```

Output

```
Sorted alphabetically:  ['Cat', 'Dog', 'Fish', 'Rabbit', 'Snake']
Elements number:  5
```

8. Dictionary

A dictionary in Python is a modifiable collection of a pair of keys and values. The keys and the values are associated, such as persons and emails, persons and their ages, an English word and its meaning in Spain or other languages. Dictionaries don't allow duplicate entries. So, the key values pair are unique.

Declaring a Dictionary in Python

The steps to declare a dictionary
- Choose an appropriate name for the dictionary.
- The pairs of key values are enclosed within a brace.
- Each key and its value in the dictionary is separated with a colon ":"
- The dictionary elements are separated with a comma, as shown in the following example.

Example 1: Finding Values by Keys

The following example declares a dictionary that consists of products as keys and prices as values. The example shows how you can print the dictionary and the prices of a specific product.

products.py

```python
# declare a dictionary
# the keys are the products and the values are the prices
products = {'milk':2.55, 'eggs':3.45, 'chips':2.15, 'bread':1.85}
# print the dictionary
print(products)
# print the prices (values) of the following products(keys)
print(products['eggs'])
print(products['bread'])
```

The output of the code is.

```
{'milk': 2.55, 'eggs': 3.45, 'chips': 2.15, 'bread': 1.85}
3.45
1.85
```

Example 2A: Print the Price of a Product

This code shows how to allow users to find the price of a product by inserting its name.

products.py

```python
# declare a dictionary
# the keys are the products and the values are the prices
products = {'milk':2.55, 'eggs':3.45, 'chips':2.15, 'bread':1.85}
product = input("Enter the name of the product: ")

price = products[product]

print("Price of ", product, " is: $",price)
```

The output shows that the user has inserted the product "chips," and the program types the price of the chips.

```
Enter the name of the product: chips
Price of  chips  is: $ 2.15
```

Suppose the user enters the product's name with different cases than the one in the dictionary.
In the following output, the user types the product "Eggs" starting with uppercase. The name Eggs in the dictionary is in lowercase. An error occurs because Python is case-sensitive.

```
KeyError: 'Eggs'
```

Example 2B: Print the Price of a Product

We improve the previous example by converting the user input into a lowercase using the lower() function, which is already explained in this book.

products.py

```python
# declare a dictionary
# the keys are the products and the values are the prices
products = {'milk':2.55, 'eggs':3.45, 'chips':2.15, 'bread':1.85}


product = input("Enter the name of the product: ")
# convert the user input to a lowercase
product = product.lower()
# the price of the product that entered by the user
price = products[product]


print("Price of", product, " is: $",price)
```

The output shows that the user entered the product eggs in uppercase, but this time, it doesn't matter because we convert the product entered by users to lowercase. When you compare two products all in lowercase, it will be found.
The user enters the "EGGS" product in this output, and the program finds it.

```
Enter the name of the product: EGGS
Price of eggs  is: $ 3.45
```

Example 3: Print the Price of a Product

How do you print all the keys, values, and pairs of keys and values using a dictionary?

products.py

```python
# declare a dictionary
# the keys are the products and the values are the prices
products = {'milk':2.55, 'eggs':3.45, 'chips':2.15, 'bread':1.85}
```

```python
print("Keys: ", products.keys())
print("Values: ", products.values())

print("----------keys-------------")
# iterating over the keys
for element in products.keys():
    print("Key: ", element)
print("----------values-------------")
# iterating over the values
for element in products.values():
    print("Value: ", element)
print("----------keys & values-------------")
# iterating over the key:vlaue pairs using .items() method
for(key, value) in products.items():
    print(key, ':', value)
```

Output

```
Keys: dict_keys(['milk', 'eggs', 'chips', 'bread'])
Values: dict_values([2.55, 3.45, 2.15, 1.85])
----------keys-------------
Key: milk
Key: eggs
Key: chips
Key: bread
----------values-------------
Value: 2.55
Value: 3.45
Value: 2.15
Value: 1.85
----------keys & values-------------
milk : 2.55
eggs : 3.45
chips : 2.15
bread : 1.85
```

Example 4: Displaying Keys and Values

The following code shows how to display all the keys and values in a dictionary. You can also iterate through all the keys and the values together or separately.

products.py

```python
# declare a dictionary
# the keys are the products and the values are the prices
products = {'milk':2.55, 'eggs':3.45, 'chips':2.15, 'bread':1.85}

# display the products (key) for the items in a sorted order
for element in sorted(products.keys()):
    print(element)
print("-------------")
# display the price (value) for the items in a sorted order
for element in sorted(products.values()):
    print(element)
```

The output of the code.

```
bread
chips
eggs
milk
-------------
1.85
2.15
2.55
3.45
```

Example 5: Adding Elements to a Dictionary

Add water and coffee to the dictionary.
water price = 1.35, coffee price = 4.55.

products.py

```python
# the keys are the products and the values are the prices
products = {'milk':2.55, 'eggs':3.45, 'chips':2.15, 'bread':1.85}


# add water with price 1.35 to the dictionary
products["water"] = 1.35
# add coffee with price 4.55 to the dictionary
products["coffee"] = 4.55
# display the products dictionary
print(products)
```

The output shows that both water and coffee with their prices are added to the dictionary products.

```
{'milk': 2.55, 'eggs': 3.45, 'chips': 2.15, 'bread': 1.85, 'water': 1.35, 'coffee': 4.55}
```

Example 6: Removing Elements From a Dictionary

Remove eggs from the dictionary by using the function pop.

- products.pop("eggs")

Remove the chips product by using the statement del.

- del products["chips"]

products.py

```python
 the keys are the products and the values are the prices
products = {'milk':2.55, 'eggs':3.45, 'chips':2.15, 'bread':1.85}


# remove eggs by using pop function
products.pop("eggs")
# remove chips by using the del keyword
del products["chips"]
# display the products dictionary
print(products)
```

The output shows that eggs and chips are removed from the products.

```
{'milk': 2.55, 'bread': 1.85}
```

Quiz 1: Number of Elements

What happens if the following code is run?

> **Notice**
> the statement len(countries) prints the number of the elements within the dictionary.

countries.py

```python
# the keys are the countries and the values are the capitals
countries = {'United States':'Washington', 'Germany':'Berlin',
'France':'Paris', 'Spain':'Madrid'}


countries.pop("United States")
del countries["France"]


print(len(countries))
```

Select the correct answer:

a. The code prints "4" to the output.

b. The code prints "8" to the output.

c. The code prints "2" to the output.

d. The code prints "3" to the output.

e. The code prints nothing to the output.

Quiz 2: Number of Elements

What happens if the following code is run?

countries.py

```python
# the keys are the countries and the values are the capitals
countries = {'United States':'Washington', 'Germany':'Berlin',
'France':'Paris', 'Spain':'Madrid'}
```

```python
print(len(countries), end= " ")
countries["United Kingdom"] = "London"
countries["Brazil"] = "Brasília"
print(len(countries))
```

Select the correct answer:

a. The code prints "4 6" to the output.

b. The code prints "4 4" to the output.

c. The code prints "6" to the output.

d. The code prints "4" to the output.

e. The code prints nothing to the output.

Quiz 3: Printing Dictionary Elements

What happens if the following code is run?

students.py

```python
# the keys are the names and the values are the ages
students = {"Edward":22, "Jack":34, "George":22}

for(key, value) in students.items():
    print(key, ':', value)
```

Select the correct answer:

a. The code prints only the student names to the output.

b. The code prints only the student ages to the output.

c. The code prints the names and the ages to the output.

d. The code prints only the name Edward and his age to the output.

e. The code prints nothing to the output.

Exercise 1: Create an English Dictionary

Write a program that allows users to enter an English word; the program displays a synonym of the word. Remember that the user could write the word all in uppercase, lowercase, or a combination of both. The program should find the synonymous if it exists in the dictionary regardless of the cases.

dictionary.py

```python
eng_dictionary = {'Happy': 'Pleased', 'Fast': 'Quick', 'Big':
'Large', 'Smart': 'Clever'}

# add your code here
```

Output 1: The user enters the word "HAPPY"

```
Enter an English word: HAPPY
The synonymous of the word Happy is Pleased
```

Output 2: The user enters the word "fast"

```
Enter an English word: fast
The synonymous of the word Fast is Quick
```

Output 3: The user enters the word "bIG"

```
Enter an English word: biG
The synonymous of the word Big is Large
```

Exercise 2: Display Laptops by Price

Develop a program enabling users to input the maximum price they're willing to spend on a laptop. The program will then exclusively display laptops priced at or below the specified price.

laptop.py

```python
laptops = {'Dell': 2200, 'HP': 1100, 'Acer': 800, 'IBM': 2300}

# add your code here
```

Output 1: The user enters the price of 2000

```
EntePlease enter a maximum price: 2000
```

```
----------Selected Laptops-------------
HP : 1100
Acer : 800
```

Output 2: The user enters the price of 1000

```
----------Selected Laptops-------------
Acer : 800
```

Answers to the Exercises

Answer Quiz 1

- The statement countries.pop("United States") removes the United States from the dictionary.
- The statement del countries["France] removes France from the dictionary.
- The statement print(len(countries)) prints the number of dictionary elements. There were originally four elements in the dictionary.
- Removing two elements remains only two elements in the dictionary.
- The correct answer is c.

Output

```
2
```

Answer Quiz 2

- The statement print(len(countries)) prints the number of elements in the dictionary, which is four.
- The statement countries["United Kingdom"] = "London" adds the UK to the dictionary.
- The statement countries["Brazil"] = Brasilia adds Brazil to the dictionary.
- The last statement print(len(countries)) prints the number of elements in the dictionary. By adding two countries, the number becomes 6.

- The correct answer is a.

Output

```
4 6
```

Answer Quiz 3

- The for loop statement prints all the keys and the values to the standard output.

The correct answer is c.

Output

```
Edward : 22
Jack : 34
George : 22
```

Answer Exercise 1

- The statement of line 1 asks the user to enter an English word.
- The statement on line 2 converts the input of the user to lowercase.
- The statement on line 3 converts the first letter of the word entered by the user to uppercase.
- All the words in the dictionary start with uppercase, and the rest of the letters are lowercase. So, the synonym will be found if the user only enters the word's correct spelling.
- The statement on line 4 finds the key's value in the dictionary entered by the user.

dictionary.py

```python
eng_dictionary = {'Happy': 'Pleased', 'Fast': 'Quick', 'Big':
'Large', 'Smart': 'Clever'}


en_word = input('Enter an English word: ')  #.....line 1
# convert the user input to lowercase
```

```
en_word = en_word.lower()                    #.....line 2
# convert the first letter to upper case
en_word = en_word.capitalize()               #.....line 3


element = eng_dictionary[en_word]            #.....line 4
print("The synonymous of the word " + en_word, "is", element)
```

Output

```
Enter an english word: HAPPY
The synonymous of the word Happy is Pleased
```

Answer Exercise 2

- Line 1 asks the user to enter the maximum price he is willing to pay for a laptop.
- The line 2 converts the price to float (decimal number)
- Line 3 is for loop iterating through the elements of the dictionary.
- Line 4 filters all the laptops that are more expensive than the maximum price of the user.
- Line 5 displays the keys and the values of the laptops. In this case, the keys are the brands, and the values are their prices.

laptops.py

```
laptops = {'Dell': 2200, 'HP': 1100, 'Acer': 800, 'IBM': 2300}


max_price =  input("Please enter a maximum price: ")     #... line 1
max_price = float(max_price)                             #... line 2


print("----------Selected Laptops-------------")
# iterating over the key:vlaue pairs using .items() method
for(key, value) in laptops.items():       #... line 3
    if(value <= max_price):               #... line 4
        print(key, ':', value)            #... line 5
```

Output: The user enters the maximum price of 1200.

```
Please enter a maximum price: 1200
----------Selected Laptops-------------
HP : 1100
Acer : 800
```

9. Functions

A Python function is a reusable block of code that can be run whenever invoked. Functions allow passing zero or more parameters and can return data. It could be used as a template that is called whenever needed. Functions are used in most programming languages, but some call it methods.

How to Declare a Function?

Every function consists of two main parts, the head and the body. The body of the function is a block code that is executed whener the function is invoked (called). To declare a function, you need to follow the next steps.

Table 1: Declaring a Function

Head of the function

Function head	Description
Head of a function	
def	Functions in Python start with the keyword def.
Function Name	A programmer can choose a proper name for the functions.
Parentheses "()"	The name of the function ends with enclosed parentheses.
Arguments or Parameters (0, 1, 2 ....)	Zero, one or more arguments could be passed through a function.
Colon ":"	The head of the function ends with a colon ":"

Body of the function

Function body	Description
Body	One or more statements to be executed

return	A function can return a value.

A function can be invoked(called) using its name and its possible arguments.

Example 1A: Company Contact

The following program displays the contact data of the company Nano Mail.

contact.py

```python
name = "Nano Mail"
phone = "033-44556677"
email = "info@nanomail.com"

print("Name:   ", name)
print("Phone: ", phone)
print("Email: ", email)
print("------------")
```

The output of this code displays all the contact data of the company Nano Mail. Suppose we need to display this contact data in many places in the application or a website.

Output

```
Name:  Nano Mail
Phone:  033-44556677
Email:  info@nanomail.com
------------
```

Copying and pasting the code to the places where you want to display the contact data is very poor. The reason is that by updating an email address, mobile number, or any other company data, the programmer should seek many places to update the data in every single place.

However, by writing a function to display the data and call the function, we can achieve the goal with one block of reusable code, as shown in the following example. In addition, duplicating the same code in various parts of the program unnecessarily increases its size.

Example 1B: Contact Data Function

Here is the function that could be invoked whenever we need it.

contact.py

```python
def compnay_contact():
    name = "Nano Mail"
    phone = "033-44556677"
    email = "info@nanomail.com"

    print("Name:   ", name)
    print("Phone: ", phone)
    print("Email: ", email)
    print("------------")
'''
call the function twice by typing its name.
'''

compnay_contact()
compnay_contact()
```

In the previous example, we called the function twice; therefore, the contact
data is printed twice in the output.

contact.py

```
Name:   Nano Mail
Phone: 033-44556677
Email: info@nanomail.com
------------
Name:   Nano Mail
Phone: 033-44556677
Email: info@nanomail.com
------------
```

Function Without Arguments

A function without arguments or parameters doesn't require any input
arguments. A function name is ended with an enclosed empty parenthesis.

Example 2: Function With No Arguments

The following function, student_name, doesn't have arguments; therefore, no arguments are passed between the parenthesis.

student_info.py

```python
def student_data():
    print("Student name is: George")


# call (invoke) the function
student_data()
```

By calling the function, the output prints the following.

```
Student name is: George
```

Function With One or More Arguments

Some functions require one or more arguments (parameters) to be passed into the parenthesis. The previous functions always print the name, George. We can make the functions more useful by printing any name the user enters; we pass the name as an input parameter.

Example 3: Function With One Argument

The following program requires one input argument. The program allows users to enter their names and prints the username.

student_info.py

```python
def student_data(name):
    print("Student name is: ", name)


username = input("Enter your name: ")
# call (invoke) the function
student_data(username)
```

The user enters the name David, and then the program prints the entered name.

```
Enter your name: David
Student name is:  David
```

Example 4: Function With Two Arguments

We can expand the previous function by passing the name and age of the user into the function as parameters.

student_info.py

```python
def student_data(name, age):
    print("Student name is: ", name)
    print("Student age is:  ", age)


username = input("Enter your name: ")
age = input("Enter your age: ")
# call (invoke) the function
student_data(username, age)
```

The users are asked to enter their names and ages.

```
Enter your name: Emma
Enter your age: 22
Student name is:  Emma
Student age is:   22
```

Functions that Return Values

A function can return a value that can be a text or a calculation result, as shown in the following example.

Example 5: Convert Currencies

The following function returns the result of calculating an amount in euros to dollars. We assume that one euro is $ 1.10.

convert_currency.py

```python
def convert_currency(amount_euro):
    amount_dollar = amount_euro * 1.10
    return amount_dollar


euro_input = input("Enter an amount in euro: ")
# convert the amount to float
euro_input = float(euro_input)
dollar_amount = convert_currency(euro_input)


# round the amount to two decimal places
print("The entered amount is: $%.2f" % dollar_amount)
```

The user enters an amount of 200 euros and the program converts it to dollars.

```
Enter an amount in euro: 200
The entered amount is: $220.00
```

Quiz 1: Function Calculator

What happens if the following code is run?

calculator.py

```python
def calculator(nr1, nr2, nr3):    # line 1
    result = nr1 + nr2 - nr3      # line 2
    return result                 # line 3
```

```
print(calculator(22, 20, 10))    # line 4
```

Select the correct answer:

a. The code prints "22" to the output.

b. The code prints "20" to the output.

c. The code prints "32" to the output.

d. The code prints "52" to the output.

e. The code prints nothing to the output.

Quiz 2: Function Calculator

What happens if the following code is run?

calculator.py

```
def calculator(nr1, nr2, nr3):   #line 1
    result = (nr1 * nr2) + nr3   #line 2
    return result                #line 3

print(calculator(2, 6, 5))       #line 4
```

Select the correct answer:

a. The code prints "17" to the output.

b. The code prints "12" to the output.

c. The code prints "13" to the output.

d. The code prints "11" to the output.

e. The code prints nothing to the output.

Quiz 3: Function Calculator

What happens if the following code is run?

text.py

```
def letters(txt1, txt2, txt3):            #line 1
    text = txt3 + txt1 + txt2 + txt3      #line 2
```

```
    return text                          #line 3

print(letters('S', 'T', 'Z'))           #line 4
```

Select the correct answer:

a. The code prints "STZ" to the output.

b. The code prints "ZST" to the output.

c. The code prints "ZTS" to the output.

d. The code prints "ZSTZ" to the output.

e. The code prints nothing to the output.

Exercise 1: Calculate Net Wage

Write a function enabling users to input their gross wages and the tax rate in their countries. The program will then calculate the net salary based on the provided gross salary and tax rate.

Output 1: The user enters a gross salary of 4000 and a tax rate of %50

```
Enter your gross salary: $4000
Enter the tax rate in your country: %50
Net wage: $2000.00
```

Output 2: The user enters a gross salary of 4000 and a tax rate of %20

```
Enter your gross salary: $4000
Enter the tax rate in your country: %20
Net wage: $3200.00
```

Exercise 2: Find the Largest Number

Create a program using a function that enables users to input three numbers one at a time. The program aims to identify and display the largest number of the provided inputs.

Output 1: The user enters the numbers 3, 4, -5

```
Enter the first number: 3
Enter the second number: 4
```

```
Enter the third number: -5
The largest is: 4
```

Output 2: The user enters the numbers 34, 76, -200

```
Enter the first number: 34
Enter the second number: 76
Enter the third number: -200
The largest is: 76
```

Output 3: The user enters the numbers 26, 26, 20

```
Enter the first number: 26
Enter the second number: 26
Enter the third number: 20
Please enter unique numbers
```

Answers to the Exercises

Answer Quiz 1

- Line 1 declares a function with three parameters.
- Line 2 calculates the result, which is the sum of the first and second parameters minus the third parameter.
- Line 3 returns the result.
- Line 4 invokes the function with the parameters 22, 20, and 10.
- The program prints the result, which is 22 + 20 - 10 = 32.
- The correct answer is c.

Output

```
32
```

Answer Quiz 2

- Line 1 declares a function with three parameters.
- Line 2 calculates the result which is (nr * nr2) + nr3

- Line 3 returns the result.
- Line 4 invokes the function with the parameters 2, 6, and 5.
- The result is (2 * 6) + 5 = 17.
- The correct answer is a.

Output

```
17
```

Answer Quiz 3

- Line 1 declares a function with three parameters.
- Line 2, the text variable concatenates the three parameters as follows.
- txt3 + txt1 + txt2 + txt3.
- Line 3 returns the text.
- Line 4 calls the function by passing the parameters S, T, and Z.
- So, the txt = Z + S + T + Z.
- The correct answer is d.

Output

```
ZSTZ
```

Answer Exercise 1

net_wage.py

```python
def net_wage(gross_salary, taxrate):
    tax_amount = (taxrate / 100) * gross_salary
    net_salary = gross_salary - tax_amount
    return net_salary


gross_wage = input("Enter your gross salary: $")
gross_wage = float(gross_wage)
country_taxrate = input("Enter the tax rate in your country: %")
taxrate = int(country_taxrate)
net_wage = net_wage(gross_wage, taxrate)
```

```
# print the net wage rounded to the nearest decimals.
print("Net wage: $%.2f" % net_wage)
```

Output

```
Enter your gross salary: $4000
Enter the tax rate in your country: %20
Net wage: $3200.00
```

Answer Exercise 2

largest.py

```python
def largest(nr1, nr2, nr3):
    if nr1 > nr2 and nr1 > nr3:
        print("The largest is:", nr1)
    elif nr2 > nr1 and nr2 > nr3:
        print("The largest is:", nr2)
    elif nr3 > nr1 and nr3 > nr2:
        print("The largest is:", nr3)
    else:
        print("Please enter unique numbers")
# ask the user to enter three numbers, one at a time
nr1 = input("Enter the first number: ")
nr2 = input("Enter the second number: ")
nr3 = input("Enter the third number: ")
# convert the numbers to integers.
nr1 = int(nr1)
nr2 = int(nr2)
nr3 = int(nr3)
# invoke the function by entering the user's numbers.
largest(nr1, nr2, nr3)
```

10. Exceptions

Exceptions may occur during the execution of a program, and it is essential to handle them appropriately, as summarized in this chapter. Ignoring an exception can lead to the termination of the program. For example, if a program attempts to divide a number by zero, it triggers an exception because the result of such a division is undefined. It is crucial to implement exception-handling mechanisms to prevent the unexpected termination of a program.

When developing a program, three types of errors may arise: syntax, runtime, and logical errors.

Syntax errors

The interpreter identifies syntax errors in Python before the program is executed. These errors occur when incorrect Python language syntax is used.

Runtime errors

If a program is free of syntax errors, it can be executed by the Python interpreter. However, during execution, the program may terminate if a runtime error occurs. Examples of runtime errors include division by zero or attempting to access an element in a list that doesn't exist.

Logical errors

Logical errors pose a challenge in debugging as they occur during program execution without causing a crash, yet they yield incorrect results. Identifying and fixing such errors requires carefully reviewing the code to specify and address the underlying issue.

Handling Exception

If an exception occurs, the program is terminated. Therefore, handling the expected exceptions during the program's runtime is essential. Python, like the other programming languages, has a method to handle exceptions by using the following keywords.

Handling Exceptions

try... except
try... except... except
try... except... else
try... finally

Divide by Zero Exception

The result of a division by zero is unknown; therefore, it causes an exception.

Example 1A: Divide by Zero

The following code tries to divide the number 20 by the variable "nr," which is zero. The program is terminated as a result of this exception.

zero_division.py

```
nr = 0
print(20/nr)
```

The output of the code is shown below.

```
ZeroDivisionError: division by zero
```

Try... Except Block

The exception of the previous example can be handled using try... except block. By handling exceptions, the following points are essential.
- The code that might cause an exception should be in a try-block.
- The try keyword ends with a colon ":".
- If the code doesn't cause an exception, the try-block is executed.
- Otherwise, the next block, which starts with the keyword "except," is executed.

Example 1B: Divide by Zero

Enclose the previous example with try... except blocks to avoid the program's termination and display a message that divides by zero and causes an exception to the user.
The try-block tries to divide 20 by zero. The program executes the exception, which informs the user of the cause of the exception.

zero_division.py

```python
nr = 0
try:
    print(20/nr)
except:
    print("The result of division by zero is unknown.")
```

The output of the above code.

```
The result of division by zero is unknown.
```

Example 1C: Divide by Zero

If you change the variable "nr" value from zero to "2". The program calculates the output as shown below.

zero_division.py

```python
nr = 2
try:
    print(20/nr)
except:
    print("The result of division by zero is unknown.")
```

The output of the above code is shown below.

```
10.0
```

Example 1D: Divide by Zero

You can also use the message automatically generated in Python using the "ZeroDivisionError" shown below. As a programmer, you can choose a name for the object that contains the automatically generated error message. We chose the name Zde, but it can be another name.

zero_division.py

```
nr = 0
try:
    print(20/nr)
except ZeroDivisionError as zde:
    print(zde)
```

The output prints the automatically generated error message.

```
division by zero
```

Type Error

If a calculation involves a string, boolean type can cause an exception because they are not numbers.

Example 2A: Type Error

The type error occurs if the program divides a string-type variable by a number. The following program is terminated because the value of the number1 variable is "40," and it is enclosed by quote. Therefore, Python sees the variable as a string.

```
number1 = "40"
number2 = 10

print(number1/number2)
```

The output prints the automatically generated error message.

```
TypeError: unsupported operand type(s) for /: 'str' and 'int'
```

Example 2B: Type Error

The type error occurs if the program divides a string-type variable by a
number. The following program is terminated because the value of the
number1 variable is "40," and it is enclosed by quote. Therefore, Python
sees the variable as a string.

type_error.py

```
number1 = "40"
number2 = 10

try:
    print(number1/number2)
except TypeError as te:
    print(te)   # automatically generated
    print("The number1 variable type is a string")
```

The output prints the automatically generated error message and the error
that the programmer determines.

```
unsupported operand type(s) for /: 'str' and 'int'
The number1 variable type is a string
```

Index Error

The index error occurs if you try to access an element index that doesn't
exist.

Example 3A: Index Error

The following element contains only four brands, from index 0 to index 3.
The code tries to print the element at index eight, which doesn't exist.

index_error.py

```
# the list contains 4 elements
list_brand = ["HP", "Dell", "IBM", "Acer"]


# try to print index 8 which doesn't exist
print(list_brand[8])
```

The output prints the automatically generated error message.

```
IndexError: list index out of range
```

Example 3B: Index Error

The following list contains only four brands, from index 0 to index 3.
The code tries to print the element at index eight, which doesn't exist.

index_error.py

```python
# the list contains 4 elements
list_brand = ["HP", "Dell", "IBM", "Acer"]

try:
    print(list_brand[8])
except IndexError as ie:
    print("Element index doesn't exist")
    # automatically generated
    print(ie)
```

The output prints the error message determined by the programmer.

```
Element index doesn't exist
list index out of range
```

Example 3C: Index Error

The following element contains only four brands, from index 0 to index 3.
The code tries to print the element at index 2.

index_error.py

```python
# the list contains 4 elements
list_brand = ["HP", "Dell", "IBM", "Acer"]

try:
    print(list_brand[2])
except IndexError as ie:
```

```python
    print("Element index doesn't exist")
    # automatically generated
    print(ie)
```

The output prints the brand at index 2, which is IBM.

```
IBM
```

Multiple Exception

Multiple exceptions are helpful if more than one exception is expected. The more specific exceptions are located at the top, while general exceptions are located at the bottom, as shown below.

Example 4A: Multiple Exceptions

The message displayed in the following example depends on the user input.

- For example, if the user enters 10, the "try-block" is executed, and the program calculates 20/10 = 10.
- If the user enters "0", the program calculates 20/0, which is unknown. Therefore, the divide by zero exception occurs.
- For example, if the user enters the letter "g," the ValueError exception occurs, and the program asks the user to enter a number.

multiple_exceptions.py

```python
number = input("Enter a number: ")

try:
    int_number = int(number)
    print("The result is: ", 20/int_number)
except ZeroDivisionError:
    print("Cannot divide by zero")
except ValueError:
    print("Please enter a number!")
```

Output 1: The user enters the number "10".

```
Enter a number: 10
```

Output 2: The user enters zero.

```
Enter a number: 0
Cannot divide by zero
```

Output 3: The user enters the letter "k."

```
Enter a number: k
Please enter a number.
```

Example 4B: Multiple Exceptions

The message displayed in the following example depends on the user input.
- If the user enters 3, for example, the "try-block" is executed, and the program prints the third element starting with "0," which is "Acer."
- If the user enters the number"9", the program cannot find index nine because it doesn't exist on the list. Therefore, the exception IndexError-block is executed.
- For example, if the user enters the letter "t," the ValueError exception occurs, and the program asks the user to enter a number.

multiple_exceptions.py

```python
# the list contains 4 elements
list_brand = ["HP", "Dell", "IBM", "Acer"]

number = input("Enter a number: ")

try:
    # convert the number to int
    int_number = int(number)
    print("The brand is:", list_brand[int_number])
except IndexError:
    print("Element",number,"doesn't exist.")
except ValueError:
    print("Please enter a number!")
```

Output 1: The user enters the number "3".

```
Enter a number: 3
The brand is: Acer
```

Output 2: The user enters 9.

```
Enter a number: 9
Element 9 doesn't exist.
```

Output 3: The user enters the letter "t."

```
Enter a number: t
Please enter a number!
```

Example 4C: Multiple Exceptions

In complicated cases, programmers can ensure handling all the exceptions by using the general "exception" shown in the code.
In the following example code, all exceptions are handled in the "exception block" regardless of the user input.

- If the user enters the number 1, the brand "Dell" is printed.
- If the user enters the number 5, the index five doesn't exist; therefore, the general exception block occurs.
- If the user enters the letter "z," for example, the same exception block occurs.

The advantage of using a general Exception is that the exception will be handled in every scenario. The disadvantage is that the message would also be general; a specific error message is more helpful for the user.

multiple_exceptions.py

```python
# the list contains 4 elements
list_brand = ["HP", "Dell", "IBM", "Acer"]


number = input("Enter a number: ")
```

```
try:
    # convert the number to int
    int_number = int(number)
    print("The brand is:", list_brand[int_number])
except Exception:
    print("Something went wrong.")
```

Output 1: The user enters the number "1".

```
Enter a number: 1
The brand is: Dell
```

Output 2: The user enters the number 5.

```
Enter a number: 5
Something went wrong.
```

Output 3: The user enters the letter "t."

```
Enter a number: z
Something went wrong.
```

Example 4D: Multiple Exceptions

A combination of specific exceptions like ZeroDivisionError, IndexError, ValueError, and the general exception is also allowed. In that case, the general exception should be at the bottom of the statements if combined with specific exceptions.

In the following example

- If the user enters the number 0, the brand "HP" is printed.
- If the user enters the number 7, the index seven doesn't exist; therefore, the IndexError occurs.
- For example, if the user enters the letter "x," the code doesn't handle the value error exception. Therefore, the general exception block is executed.

multiple_exceptions.py

```python
# the list contains 4 elements
list_brand = ["HP", "Dell", "IBM", "Acer"]

number = input("Enter a number: ")

try:
    # convert the number to int
    int_number = int(number)
    print("The brand is:", list_brand[int_number])
except IndexError:
    print("Element doesn't exist.")
except Exception:
    print("Something went wrong.")
```

Output 1: The user enters the number "0".

```
Enter a number: 0
The brand is: HP
```

Output 2: The user enters the number 7.

```
Enter a number: 7
Element doesn't exist.
```

Output 3: The user enters the letter "x".

```
Enter a number: x
Something went wrong.
```

The Keyword Finally

The finally-block is located at the end of the exception blocks and is always executed. No matter what the user input is, the finally-block is executed.

Example 5: Finally Keyword

We add the finally-block to the previous example. It doesn't matter whether the try-block or any of the except-blocks is executed. The finally-block is always executed; see the three possible outputs of the following code.

finally_key.py

```python
# the list contains 4 elements
```

```python
list_brand = ["HP", "Dell", "IBM", "Acer"]

number = input("Enter a number: ")

try:
    # convert the number to int
    int_number = int(number)
    print("The brand is:", list_brand[int_number])
except IndexError:
    print("Element doesn't exist.")
except Exception:
    print("Something went wrong.")
finally:
    print("The finally-block is always executed.")
```

Output 1: The user enters the number "3".

```
Enter a number: 3
The brand is: Acer
The finally-block is always executed.
```

Output 2: The user enters the number "9".

```
Enter a number: 9
Element doesn't exist.
The finally-block is always executed.
```

Output 3: The user enters the letter "y."

```
Enter a number: y
Something went wrong.
The finally-block is always executed.
```

Quiz 1: Zero Division Exception

What happens if the following code is run?

except.py

```python
try:
    nr = 6/0
    print("x")
```

```
except ZeroDivisionError:
    print("N")
except Exception:
    print("P")
```

Select the correct answer:

a. The code prints "XN" to the output.

b. The code prints "XNP" to the output.

c. The code prints "N" to the output.

d. The code prints "XP" to the output.

e. The code prints nothing to the output.

Quiz 2: Index Exception

What happens if the following code is run?

except.py

```
cars = ["Audi", "Ford", "Jeep", "Volvo", "Toyota"]
try:
    car = cars[7]
    print("Kia ")
except IndexError:
    print("Tesla ")
except Exception:
    print("BMW ")
```

Select the correct answer:

a. The code prints "Kia" to the output.

b. The code prints "Volvo" to the output.

c. The code prints "Volvo Kia" to the output.

d. The code prints "Tesla" to the output.

e. The code prints "BMW" to the output.

f. The code prints nothing to the output.

Quiz 3: Exception

What happens if the following code is run?

except.py

```
cars = ["Audi", "Ford", "Jeep", "Volvo", "Toyota"]
try:
    car = cars["z"]
    print("Kia", end = " ")
except IndexError:
    print("Tesla", end = " ")
except Exception:
    print("BMW", end = " ")
finally:
    print("Jeep", end = " ")
```

Select the correct answer:

a. The code prints "Jeep" to the output.

b. The code prints "Tesla Jeep" to the output.

c. The code prints "Tesla" to the output.

d. The code prints "BMW Jeep" to the output.

e. The code prints "BMW" to the output.

f. The code prints nothing to the output.

Exercise 1: Index Exception

Create a program that enables users to input an index corresponding to the list provided below:

- If the user inputs a valid index, the program will display the item associated with that index.
- If the user inputs an index that does not exist, the program will notify the user of the non-existent index.

- If the user inputs a letter or non-numeric input, a prompt will guide them to enter a valid number.
- Following the output, the user will always receive a notification confirming the successful execution of the program.

The following are the possible outputs of the program.

except.py

```
items = ["Notebook", "Sunglasses", "Smartphone", "Headphones",
"Backpack"]
# add your code here
```

Output 1: The user enters the number 3

```
Enter the index of an item: 3
The item at index 3 is: Headphones
The program executed successfully.
```

Output 2: The user enters the number 11

```
Enter the index of an item: 11
The index 11 is out of range.
The program executed successfully.
```

Output 3: The user enters the letter "y"

```
Enter the index of an item: y
Invalid input. Please enter a valid index.
The program executed successfully.
```

Exercise 2: Arithmetic Exception

Develop a program that allows users to input two numbers, specifying one as the numerator and the other as the denominator:

- Upon receiving valid numerical inputs, the program calculates the result of the division operation between the numerator and denominator.
- In case of incorrect input(s), the program guides the user to enter valid numbers.

- If the user inputs zero as the denominator, the program provides guidance, informing the user that the result is indeterminate.

Output 1: The user enters the numbers 22 and 2

```
Enter the numerator: 22
Enter the denominator: 2
The result of 22.0 / 2.0 is: 11.0
Program executed successfully.
```

Output 2: The user enters the numbers 41 and 0

```
Enter the numerator: 41
Enter the denominator: 0
Zero is not allowed as a denominator.
Program executed successfully.
```

Output 3: The user enters R as a numerator.

```
Enter the numerator: R
Please enter a valid input.
Program executed successfully.
```

Output 4: The user enters 30 as a numerator and the letter "K"as a denominator.

```
Enter the numerator: 30
Enter the denominator: K
Please enter a valid input.
Program executed successfully.
```

Answers to the Exercises

Answer Quiz 1

- The statement 6/0 causes a zero division error.
- The program executes the ZeroDivisionError and the letter "N" is printed to the standard output.

The correct anser is c.

Output

N

Answer Quiz 2

- The statement car = car[7] causes the exception IndexError; therefore, the brand Tesla is printed to the output.

The correct answer is d.

Output

```
Tesla
```

Answer Quiz 3

- The statement car = car["z"] tries to access the index "z" in the list, which should be a number.
- The general Exception occurs, and "BMW" is printed to the output.
- The finally-block is always executed; therefore, the brand "Jeep" is also printed on the output.

The correct answer is d.

Output

```
BMW Jeep
```

Answer Exercise 1

items.py

```python
items = ["Notebook", "Sunglasses", "Smartphone", "Headphones",
"Backpack"]

try:
    item_index = input("Enter the index of an item: ")
    item_index = int(item_index)
    print("The item at index", item_index, "is:",
```

```
items[item_index])
except IndexError:
    print("The index", item_index, "is out of range.")
except ValueError:
    print("Invalid input. Please enter a valid index.")
finally:
    print("The program executed successfully.")
```

Output 1: The user enters the number 3

```
Enter the index of an item: 3
The item at index 3 is: Headphones
The program executed successfully.
```

Output 2: The user enters the number 11

```
Enter the index of an item: 11
The index 11 is out of range.
The program executed successfully.
```

Output 3: The user enters the letter "y"

```
Enter the index of an item: y
Invalid input. Please enter a valid index.
The program executed successfully.
```

Answer Exercise 2

calculator.py

```
try:
    numerator = float(input("Enter the numerator: "))
    denominator = float(input("Enter the denominator: "))

    result = numerator / denominator
    print("The result of" ,numerator,"/",denominator,"is:",
result)

except ZeroDivisionError:
```

```
    print("Zero is not allowed as a denominator.")
except ValueError as ve:
    print("Please enter a valid input. ")


finally:
    print("Program executed successfully.")
```

Output 1: The user enters the numbers 22 and 2

```
Enter the numerator: 22
Enter the denominator: 2
The result of 22.0 / 2.0 is: 11.0
Program executed successfully.
```

Output 2: The user enters the numbers 41 and 0

```
Enter the numerator: 41
Enter the denominator: 0
Zero is not allowed as a denominator.
Program executed successfully.
```

Output 3: The user enters R as a numerator.

```
Enter the numerator: R
Please enter a valid input.
Program executed successfully.
```

Output 4: The user enters 30 as a numerator and the letter "K" as a denominator.

```
Enter the numerator: 30
Enter the denominator: K
Please enter a valid input.
Program executed successfully.
```

11. Import Random

Many modules are already written in Python, and their code is available for programmers to import. By importing a module, the code will be available in the module where you are importing it.

You can import a module into your program by using the statements below.

- import (module name): Imports all the functionalities of the module. For example, import random and import math
- from (module name) import (function name): Imports the specific function. An example is from random import randrage

Random Randrage

You can import the random module in Python by using the keyword import. The function "randrange" within the module random allows two parameters. The first parameter is the start number, which is included. The stop number, or the second one, is the number that is excluded from the random number.

Example 1: randrage(2, 7) possible random numbers are 2, 3, 4, 5, 6.

Example 1: Import Random

If the following program is run, the randrage(1, 4) decides the range of the generated random number. Number one is included, while number four is excluded. A number from 1 to 4 is randomly displayed each time you run the program. The possible numbers are 1, 2, and 3.

random_nr.py

```
# integers randrange(start included, stop excluded)
from random import randrange
random_nr = randrange(1, 4)
print(random_nr)
```

Output 1: The generated random number is 2.

```
2
```

Output 2: The generated random number is 1.

```
1
```

Example 2A: Dice

If the following program is run, the randrage(1, 7) determines the range of the generated random number. The possible numbers that are randomly generated are: 1, 2, 3, 4, 5, 6.

dice.py

```python
# a dice range is from one to six
from random import randrange
random_nr = randrange(1, 7)
print(random_nr)
```

Output: The generated random number is four, and the possibilities are 1, 2, 3, 4, 5 and 6.

```
4
```

Example 2B: Two Dices

The following program declares the dice, dice1, and dice2.
Each time you run the program, two random numbers from one to six are printed..

dice.py

```python
# a dice range is from one to six
```

```python
from random import randrange
dice1 = randrange(1, 7)
dice2 = randrange(1, 7)
print(dice1, "", dice2)
```

Output: The generated random numbers.

```
5 6
```

Random Choice

The choice function allows the random selection of one element within a list.

Example 3A: Select Cards

The following program declares a list with the card elements. The choice function allows you to select a card randomly.

cards.py

```python
from random import choice
cards = ["clubs", "Diamonds", "Hearts", "Spades"]
selected_card = choice(cards)

print("Randomly selected card: ", selected_card)
```

Output: The Heart card is selected randomly.

```
Randomly selected card:  Hearts
```

Example 3B: Select Cards and Card Values

The following program declares a list with the card elements and values. The choice function allows you to select a card randomly.

cards.py

```python
from random import choice
cards = ["clubs", "Diamonds", "Hearts", "Spades"]
card_value = ["Ace", 2, 3, 4, 5, 6, 7, 8, 9, 10, "Jack", "Queen",
"King"]
selected_card = choice(cards)
selected_card_value = choice(card_value)


print("Randomly selected card: ",
selected_card_value,"of",selected_card)
```

Output: By running the program, a card is selected randomly.

```
Randomly selected card:  Queen of Hearts
```

Random Shuffle

The shuffle function allows to change the order of the list elements

Example 3C: Shuffle Cards

The following program declares a list of cards. The shuffle function randomly changes the order of the card elements within the list, as shown in the program's output.

shuffle.py

```python
from random import shuffle
cards = ["clubs", "Diamonds", "Hearts", "Spades"]
# change the cards order randomly
shuffle(cards)
print(cards)
```

Output 1: The order of the cards is changed randomly.

```
['Hearts', 'clubs', 'Diamonds', 'Spades']
```

By rerunning the program, the order is changed again randomly.

```
['Spades', 'clubs', 'Diamonds', 'Hearts']
```

Quiz 1: Random

What happens if the following code is run?

random.py

```
from random import randrange
random_nr = randrange(1, 2)
print(random_nr)
```

Select the correct answer:

a. The code prints "1 or 2" to the output.

b. The code prints "1" to the output.

c. The code prints "1, 2 or 3" to the output.

d. The code prints "2" to the output.

e. The code prints nothing to the output.

Quiz 2: Random

Which values should be passed to the randrange function
to select a random number from 10 to 20, inclusive?

random.py

```
from random import randrange
random_nr = randrange(0, 0)
print(random_nr)
```

Select the correct answer:

a. The values should be randrange(9, 21).

b. The values should be randrage(10, 21).

c. The values should be randrage(10, 20).

d. The values should be randrage(9, 20).

e. The code prints nothing to the output.

Exercise 1: Lottery

Create a program allowing users to shuffle the names in the list below. Upon executing the program, the names order is selected randomly. The winners are determined based on the following ranking:

- The first randomly selected name wins one million dollars.
- The second chosen random name wins 500 thousand dollars.
- The third randomly selected name wins 100 thousand dollars.

lottery.py

```
from random import shuffle
names = ["Emma", "David", "Jack", "George", "Ronald", "Vera",
"Bruce"]

# add the rest of your code here.
```

The output of the program is shown below. Remember that the winners will be randomly different each time you run the program.

```
The names randomly:
['Vera', 'Emma', 'Bruce', 'Ronald', 'David', 'Jack', 'George']
The winner of one million dollars is: Vera
The winner of 500 thousand dollars is: Emma
The winner of 100 thousand dollars is: Bruce
```

Exercise 2: Card Game

Write a program randomly assigning a card from a predefined list, using the provided lists for both cards and their corresponding values.

```
cards = ["clubs", "Diamonds", "Hearts", "Spades"]
card_values = [2, 3, 4, 5, 6, 7, 8, 9, 10, 'Jack', 'Queen',
'King', 'Ace']

# add your code here.
```

The output of the program is shown below. Remember that a random card is selected each time you run the program.

Output 1

```
Your selected card is:  Ace of clubs
```

Output 2

```
Your selected card is:  4 of Diamonds
```

Output 3

```
Your selected card is:  4 of clubs
```

Answers to the Exercises

Answer Quiz 1

- The statement random_nr = randrage(1, 2). The start number is "1," which is included, but the stop number is "2", which is excluded from the generated random numbers.
- The correct answer is that the number 1 is always selected.

The correct answer is b.

Answer Quiz 2

- The statement randrage(10, 21). The start number is "10," which is included, but the stop number is "21", which is excluded from the generated random numbers.
- The range 10 to 21 generates random numbers from 10 to 20.

The correct answer is b.

Answer Exercise 1

lottery.py

```python
from random import shuffle
```

```python
names = ["Emma", "David", "Jack", "George", "Ronald", "Vera",
"Bruce"]

shuffle(names)

print("The names randomly: \n",names)

print("The winner of one million dollars is:", names[0])
print("The winner of 500 thousand dollars is:", names[1])
print("The winner of 100 thousand dollars is:", names[2])
```

The output of the program is shown below. Remember that the winners will be randomly different each time you run the program.

```
The names randomly:
 ['Vera', 'Emma', 'Bruce', 'Ronald', 'David', 'Jack', 'George']
The winner of one million dollars is: Vera
The winner of 500 thousand dollars is: Emma
The winner of 100 thousand dollars is: Bruce
```

Answer Exercise 2

```python
from random import choice

cards = ["clubs", "Diamonds", "Hearts", "Spades"]
card_values = [2, 3, 4, 5, 6, 7, 8, 9,  10, 'Jack', 'Queen',
'King', 'Ace']
# select a random card
random_card = choice(cards)
# select a random card value
random_card_value = choice(card_values)

print("Your selected card is: ", random_card_value, "of",
random_card)
```

The output of the program is shown below. Remember that a random card is selected each time you run the program.

Output 1

```
Your selected card is:  Ace of clubs
```

Output 2

```
Your selected card is:  4 of Diamonds
```

Output 3

```
Your selected card is:  4 of clubs
```

12. Date and Time

Python enables the management of date and time, including the retrieval of the current date and time, by importing the date or the datetime module.

Example 1: Printing The Current Date

The output of the program depends on the current date.

today.py

```python
from datetime import date
today = date.today()
print("Today: ", today)
```

Output of the program

```
Today:  2024-03-04
```

Example 2A: Printing a Selected Date

You can use any date you want to print; the order is year, month, and day.

selected_date.py

```python
from datetime import date
# the order of the date is year, month, and day.
date2 = date(2023, 4, 22)
print("Date: ", date2)
```

Output of the program

```
Date:  2023-04-22
```

Example 2B: Printing a Selected Date

You can use any date you want to print by determining the day, month, and year, as shown below.

selected_date.py

```python
from datetime import date
date2 = date(day=25, month=3, year=2017)
print("Date: ", date2)
```

Output of the program

```
Date:  2017-03-25
```

Example 2C: Updating a Selected Date

You can update any date using the function replace, as shown in the following example.

replace_date.py

```python
from datetime import date
current_date = date(day=25, month=3, year=2018)
print("Selected date: ", current_date)


new_date = current_date.replace(month = 7, year=2023)
print("New date: ", new_date)
```

Output of the program

```
Selected date:  2018-03-25
New date:  2023-07-25
```

Table 1: Format Date Object

By using the following symbols, you can change the format of the date to the US, Europe, or any style you wish.

Symbol	Description
%a	Sun, Mon ..
%A	Sunday, Monday....

%d	01, 02, ...31
%b	Jan, Feb ... Dec
%B	January, February ...December
%m	01, 02, ... 12
%y	00, 02, 99
%Y	1900, 1998, 2018

Example 3A: Formatting Date

You can change the date format to the US, Europe, or any style you wish.

format_date.py

```python
from datetime import date
current_date = date(year=2024, month=2, day=19)
format1 = current_date.strftime("%B %d %Y")
print("Format 1: ", format1)


format2 = current_date.strftime("%d-%b-%y")
print("Format 2: ", format2)


format3 = current_date.strftime("%m/%d/%Y")
print("Format 3: ", format3)
```

Output of the program

```
Format 1:  February 19 2024
Format 2:  19-Feb-24
Format 2:  02/19/2024
```

Example 3B: Formatting The Current Date

You can change the date format of today as shown below.

format_today.py

```python
from datetime import date
```

```python
# Get the current date
today = date.today()

# Format the date (MM/DD/YYYY)
format = today.strftime("%m/%d/%Y")


print("American Format:", format)
```

Output of the program

```
American Format: 03/14/2024
```

Table 2: Format Time Object

Using the following symbols, you can change the time format to 24 hours or AM or PM style.

Symbol	Description
%H	hour in 24-hour clock
%I	Hour in 12-hour clock
%p	AM or PM
%M	minutes
%S	seconds

Example 4: Formatting Time

You can change the time format to any style you wish.

format_date.py

```python
from datetime import time
time1 = time(hour=22, minute=2, second=30)
format1 = time1.strftime("%I:%M:%S  %p")
```

```python
print("Format 1 (PM AM): ", format1)

format2 = time1.strftime("%H:%M:%S")
print("Format 2 (24 hours): ", format2)
```

Output of the program

```
Format 1 (PM AM):  10:02:30  PM
Format 2 (24 hours):  22:02:30
```

Example 5: Formatting Date and Time

You can change the format of the date and time simultaneously.

format_date.py

```python
from datetime import datetime
current_date = datetime(year=2024, month=6, day=18, hour=23,
minute=20, second=47)
format1 = current_date.strftime("%B %d %Y  %I:%M:%S %p")
print("Format 1: ", format1)

format2 = current_date.strftime("%d-%b-%y %H:%M:%S")
print("Format 2: ", format2)

format3 = current_date.strftime("%m/%d/%Y %H:%M:%S")
print("Format 3: ", format3)
```

Output of the program

```
Format 1:  June 18 2024  11:20:47 PM
Format 2:  18-Jun-24 23:20:47
Format 3:  06/18/2024 23:20:47
```

Quiz 1: Date

What happens if the following code is run?

today.py

```python
from datetime import date
current_date = date(year=2024, month=7, day=10)
```

```
format = current_date.strftime("%B %d %Y")
print(format)
```

Select the correct answer:

a. The code prints "2024 july 10" to the output.

b. The code prints "10 July 2024" to the output.

c. The code prints "07 10 24" to the output.

d. The code prints "July 10 2024" to the output.

e. The code prints nothing to the output.

Quiz 2: Date

What happens if the following code is run?

fixed_date.py

```
from datetime import date
current_date = date(year=2024, month=4, day=21)


format = current_date.strftime("%m %d %Y")
print(format)
```

Select the correct answer:

a. The code prints "04 21 2024" to the output.

b. The code prints "21 April 2024" to the output.

c. The code prints "April 21 24" to the output.

d. The code prints "April 21 2024" to the output.

e. The code prints nothing to the output.

Exercise 1: Registration Date

Upon registering on your website, the system automatically captures and saves the registration date and time. Develop a program that allows users to enter their names, and the program displays the user's name alongside the current registration date and time.

Output: The user enters Jack, and the program automatically prints the current date and time.

```
Enter your name: Jack
Jack's registration was recorded on
03/04/2024 At 08:20:54 PM
```

Exercise 2: Current Date and Time

Write a program that prints the current date and time in the following format. Use the previous tables 1 and 2 by formatting the date and time.

Output

```
The current date and time is: Monday 03/04/2024 20:22:03
```

Answers to the Exercises

Answer Quiz 1

- Read the symbols %B %d %Y in the table 1 format date.

The correct answer is d.

Answer Quiz 2

- Read the symbols %m %d %Y in the table 1 format date.

The correct answer is a.

Answer Exercise 1

registration.py

```python
from datetime import datetime


# get the current date and time
now = datetime.now()
# format the date in (MM/DD/YYYY)
```

```python
format = now.strftime("%m/%d/%Y At %I:%M:%S %p")

name = input("Enter your name: ")
print(name,"'s registration was recorded on\n",format, sep="")
```

Output: The user enters David, and the program automatically prints the current date and time.

```
Enter your name: David
David's registration was recorded on
03/04/2024 At 08:23:11 PM
```

Answer Exercise 2

current_datetime.py

```python
from datetime import datetime

# Get the current date and time
now = datetime.now()
# Format the date in (MM/DD/YYYY)
format = now.strftime("%A %m/%d/%Y %H:%M:%S")

print("The current date and time is:", format)
```

Output

```
The current date and time is: Monday 02/26/2024 19:08:26
```

13. Files Directories and OS

In online shopping, downloading invoices directly is a common practice. These invoices are automatically generated by the programming language operated by the software or website. Python facilitates the creation and manipulation of files through some essential functions.

How to create directories?

When creating any directories, you have to define the path where you want to make it, and you need to import the Python module os, which allows users to handle directories. In the subsequent example, we create directories in the exact location as the Python code. You can customize the path to your preferred location to generate directories in alternative paths, such as the root of the "C" or "D" drive.

Example 1A: Creating a Directory

You can create a directory by running a piece of code. The program aims not to see some output, but the map "_generated_map" is created on the path where the Python code "make_dir.py" exists on your computer.
By passing the path to the function mkdir in the module os, we can create a map in that path.

> **Notice**
> After running the following code, check the path where your Python code "make_dir.py" exists, and you will see that the map "_generated_map" is automatically created there.

make_dir.py

```
import os
# you can choose another path
path_dir = "_generated_map"
```

```
os.mkdir(path_dir)
```

Example 1B: Creating a Sub-Directory

You can create a subdirectory "submap" within the directory "_generated_map" by running the following code.

> **Notice**
>
> This code creates the map "_generated_map" and the subdirectory "submap." within it. If the directory "_generated_map" is already created on your path, you will see an error because you cannot create two directories with the same name on the same path.

Delete the directory "_generated_map" first and run the following code.

make_dir.py

```python
import os

path_dir = "_generated_files"
os.mkdir(path_dir)

path_subdir = path_dir + "/submap"
os.mkdir(path_subdir)
```

Example 1C: Checking the Existence of a Directory

It is efficient to check whether a directory exists because you can prevent errors if it exists and you want to make another one with the same name. The following example shows a message that the directory exists if it is available; otherwise, it creates the directory in the given path.

make_dir.py

```python
import os

path_dir = "_generated_map"
```

```python
# check whether the directory already exists
if os.path.exists(path_dir):
    print("A directory with that name already exists.")
else:
    os.mkdir(path_dir)
    print("The directory has been successfully created.")
```

Output: If the directory already exists.

```
A directory with that name already exists.
```

Output: If the directory is not created yet.

```
The directory has been successfully created.
```

How to remove directories?

When removing a directory, it is essential to specify both the path and the directory's name. The os module is required, as the function responsible for removing directories in Python is called rmdir and is included within the os module.

Example 2: Removing a Directory

In the following example, if the directory in the given path doesn't exist, the program creates one. But if the directory already exists, the program removes it.

remove_dir.py

```python
import os


path_dir = "_generated_map"
# check whether the directory already exists
if os.path.exists(path_dir):
    # remove the directory if exists
    os.rmdir(path_dir)
    print("The directory is removed")
```

```
else:
    # create a new directory with the given name
    os.mkdir(path_dir)
    print("The directory has been successfully created.")
```

Output: If the directory doesn't exist.

The directory has been successfully created.

Output: If the directory already exists.

The directory is removed

Creating and Working With Files

How to create, delete, read, and write files?

Table 1: File Modes

Here is a list of the different modes of opening a file:

Mode	Description
x	Opens the file exclusively for creation in Python 3, failing if the file already exists.
r	Opens a file in read-only mode with the file pointer positioned at the beginning of the file.
r+	Opens a file for reading and writing, positioning the file pointer at the beginning of the file.
w	Opens a file in write-only mode, overwriting the content if the file exists. Creates a new file if it doesn't exist.
w+	Opens a file for writing and reading, overwriting the content if the file exists. Creates a new file for reading and writing if it doesn't exist.
a	Opens a file in append mode, positioning the file pointer at the end if the file exists. Creates a new file for writing if it

	doesn't exist.
a+	Opens a file for both appending and reading, positioning the file pointer at the end if the file exists. Opens the file in append mode. Creates a new file for reading and writing if it doesn't exist.

Example 3: Create a File

The following program creates an empty "MyFile.txt" text within the given path, the path where the Python code exists.

file_create.py

```python
import os
path_dir = "MyFile.txt"
# check whether the file doesn't exist
if not os.path.exists(path_dir):
    # create an empty text file called MyFile.txt
    file = open(path_dir, "x")
    print("The file is created.")
    file.close()
else:
    print("The file already exists.")
```

The output of the program if the file doesn't exist.

```
The file is created.
```

The output of the program if the file already exists.

```
The file already exists.
```

Writing to an Existing File

You can add one of the parameters "w" or "a" to write to an existing file.

Mode	Description
w (write)	Overwrites any existing content of the file.
a (append)	Appends text to the end of the file.

Example 4: Write to a File

The following program opens the file MyFile.txt and writes the quote1 to it.

file_writer.py

```
path_dir = "MyFile.txt"
file_writer = open(path_dir, "w")
quote1 = "Quote 1: There Are No Limits. "
# writes the text to the file
file_writer.write(quote1)


file_writer = open(path_dir, "a")
quote2 = "Quote2: Energy Flows Where Attention Goes."
# appends the quote2 to the end of the file content.
file_writer.write(quote2)
# close the file
file_writer.close()
```

The file MyFile.txt is created on the given path by running the program.
Then, both quotes are written to the file.

The file is created.

Notice

Open the created file "MyFile.txt," where the code "file_writer.py" exists.
You will see that both quotes are written into the file automatically.

Reading an Existing File

By reading a single line or the lines separately, you can call the function readline.

Example 5A: Read a File

To read a file, we first create one named "MyFile.txt" in the root where the Python code exists. Before reading the file, please run the following code that creates it and writes some texts into it.

file_writer.py

```
path_dir = "MyFile.txt"

file_writer = open(path_dir, "w")
text = ("United States - Washington. \n"
        "Germany - Berlin. \n"
        "India - New Delhi. \n"
        "Brazil - Brasília.\n"
        "Spain - Madrid.\n")
file_writer.write(text)
file_writer.close()
```

The following program opens MyFile.txt and then reads the first three lines of the file's content.

file_readline.py

```
# open the file to read the first three lines
file_reader = open("MyFile.txt")
print(file_reader.readline())
print(file_reader.readline())
print(file_reader.readline())
file_reader.close()
```

The file MyFile.txt is created on the given path by running the previous program. The output of the following code prints the first three lines of the file content MyFile.txt.

```
United States - Washington.

Germany - Berlin.

India - New Delhi.
```

Open File for Reading

We can read an existing file by passing the "r" parameter to the open function.

"r" - opens a file for reading only. The pointer is at the beginning of the file.

Example 5B: Read a File

The following program opens the file MyFile.txt to read it. If you write this code in another path, copy the previously generated file MyFile.txt to the root where this code exists on your computer.

file_read.py

```python
path_dir = "MyFile.txt"


# open the file for reading the first line
file_reader = open(path_dir, "r")
# read the file
print(file_reader.read())
file_reader.close()
```

The output prints the content of the file.

```
United States - Washington.
Germany - Berlin.
India - New Delhi.
Brazil - Brasília.
Spain - Madrid.
```

Example 5C: Readline Loop

The following program opens the file MyFile.txt to read it.

file_read.py

```python
file_reader = open(path_dir, "r")
nr = 0
while True:
    nr += 1
    # the next line from the file
    line = file_reader.readline()
    print(line)
    # if the rest of the file is empty, the end of it is reached
    if not line:
        break
file_reader.close()
```

By running the program, the output prints the content of the file.

```
United States - Washington.

Germany - Berlin.

India - New Delhi.

Brazil - Brasília.

Spain - Madrid.
```

Example 6: List Files and Directories

The following program prints the list of the directories within the root where the Python code "list_maps.py" exists.

list_maps.py

```python
import os
print(os.listdir())
```

Output

```
['list_maps_files.py']
```

Example 7: Which Operating System

The following program displays the name of the operating system on your computer. In my case, the installed operating system is "Linux." The result depends on which operating system is installed on your computer.

os_name.py

```
# you need to import the module sys
import sys
print(sys.platform)
```

Output

```
linux
```

Example 8: Current Working Directories

The following program displays the exact path of where your Python code "current_dir.py" exists. Remember, the output on your computer can be different.

current_dir.py

```
import os
print(os.getcwd())
```

The following is the path's output on my computer, but yours could be different.

```
workspace_python/learn_python/_13_files/examples/_08_current_root
```

Quiz 1: Creating Maps

What happens if the following code is run?

map.py

```
import os

path_dir1 = "map1"
os.mkdir(path_dir1)

path_dir2 = path_dir1 + "/map2"
os.mkdir(path_dir2)
```

Select all the correct answers:

a. The code creates "map1" within "map2".

b. The code creates "map2" within "map1".

c. The code creates "map1" within the execution path of this code.

d. The code creates "map1" and "map2" separately.

e. The code causes an error.

Quiz 2: Creating and Writing Into a File

When executing the following code, it generates the file 'MyFile.txt.'
What content is readable inside the file?

file.py

```
path_dir = "MyFile.txt"

file1 = open(path_dir, "w")
q1 = "In the middle of difficulties lies opportunities." # Einstein
q2 = "What we think, we become." # Buddha
file1.close()

file1 = open(path_dir, "w")
file1.write(q2)
file1.close()
```

Select all the correct answers:

a. The content of the file is only "quote1."

b. The content of the file is only "quote2."

c. The content of the file is "quote1" and "quote2."

d. The content of the file is empty.

e. The code causes an error.

Exercise 1: Movie List

Create a list within a program named 'movies.py' and write the following movie titles in the list:
The Godfather, Wall Street, The Pianist, and The Matrix.
When you run the program, the content of the file will be displayed in the output as follows:

Output

```
The Godfather
Wall Street
The Pianist
The Matrix
```

Exercise 2: Courses Information

Create a program that generates files for each item in a given list. The files should be named course_1.txt, course_2.txt, and so on. Each file should contain the text 'Course Info.' followed by the respective course information from the given list.
courses = ["Python: $3000", "Java: $3500", "HTML: $2900", "SQL: $2800"]

After running the program, the files course_1.txt, course_2.txt, course_3.txt, and course_4.txt.
The following shows the content of the four files that are generated automatically.

course_1.txt

```
Course Info
Python: $3000
```

course_2.txt

```
Course Info
Java: $3500
```

course_3.txt

```
Course Info
HTML: $2900
```

course_4.txt

```
Course Info
SQL: $2800
```

Answers to the Exercises

Answer Quiz 1

The following code explains all the lines of the quiz code.

map.py

```python
import os

path_dir1 = "map1"
# creates 'map1' in the directory where the 'map.py' code is
located.
os.mkdir(path_dir1)
# the 'map2' is added to the map1 and becomes a submap of map1
path_dir2 = path_dir1 + "/map2"
# creates the map2 within map1
os.mkdir(path_dir2)
```

The correct answers are b and c.

Answer Quiz 2

The following code explains all the lines of the quiz code.

```
path_dir = "MyFile.txt"
'''
opens the file 'MyFile.txt' for writing,
creating it if it doesn't exist.
'''
file1 = open(path_dir, "w")
# A. Einstein
q1 = "In the middle of difficulties lies opportunities."
q2 = "What we think, we become." # Buddha
# writes q1 to the file
file1.write(q1)
# closes the file
file1.close()
# opens the file again
file1 = open(path_dir, "w")
# overwrites the content
file1.write(q2)
# closes the file
file1.close()
```

The correct answer is b.

Answer Exercise 1

Here is the code of the exercise with explanations.

movies.py

```
movies = "The Godfather\n" + "Wall Street\n" + "The Pianist\n" +
"The Matrix\n"

path = "movie_list.txt"
# opens the file for writing and creates it if it doesn't exist
file = open(path, "w")
# writes the movies into the file
file.write(movies)
# opens the file for reading
file = open(path, "r")
```

```python
# reads the file
print(file.read())
# close the file
file.close()
```

Answer Exercise 2

Here is the code of the exercise.

course.py

```python
courses = ["Python: $3000", "Java: $3500", "HTML: $2900", "SQL: $2800"]
for i in range(len(courses)):
    # generate the file name
    path = "course_" + str(i+1) +".txt"
    # open the file for writing and create it if it doesn't exist
    f = open(path, "w")
    #  write the course information into the file
    f.write("Course Info\n")
    f.write(courses[i])
f.close()
```

After running the program, open the four created files.

course_1.txt

```
Course Info
Python: $3000
```

course_2.txt

```
Course Info
Java: $3500
```

course_3.txt

```
Course Info
HTML: $2900
```

course_4.txt

```
Course Info
SQL: $2800
```

TABLE OF INDEX

Alphabetical Index